Gordon Ramsay
Quick and Delicious

Gordon Ramsay

Quick and Delicious

HODDER &
STOUGHTON

First published in Great Britain in 2019
by Hodder & Stoughton
An Hachette UK company

A CIP catalogue record for this title is available from the British Library.

Hardback ISBN 978 1 529 32543 0
eBook ISBN 978 1 529 32544 7

Editorial Director: Nicky Ross
Project Editor: Natalie Bradley
Editor: Camilla Stoddart
Copy-editor: Patricia Burgess
Design and Art Direction: Peter Dawson, Alice Kennedy-Owen,
gradedesign.com
Photographer: Louise Hagger
Food Stylist: Nicole Herft
Prop Stylists: Alexander Breeze and Louie Waller
Senior Production Controller: Susan Spratt

Colour origination by Altaimage
Printed and bound by Firmengruppe APPL, aprinta druck,
Wemding, Germany

Hodder & Stoughton policy is to use papers that are natural, renewable
and recyclable products and made from wood grown in sustainable
forests. The logging and manufacturing processes are expected
to conform to the environmental regulations of the country of origin.

Hodder & Stoughton Ltd
Carmelite House
50 Victoria Embankment
London EC4Y 0DZ

Contents

Introduction	7
My Advice for Faster, Better Cooking	8
Kit List	10
Shortcuts to Flavour	12
Time-saving Ingredients	13

Soups and Salads — 14

Fish and Shellfish — 38

Poultry — 74

Meat — 102

Meat-free Mains — 136

Pasta, Rice and Grains — 164

Dips and Sides — 192

Puddings — 214

Index	246
Acknowledgements	255
Metric/Imperial Conversion Chart	256

Introduction

Speed is a vital ingredient in restaurant kitchens: it is essential to get the food out quickly, or people just won't come back. Although things are less pressurised at home, there is a lot to learn from professional chefs when it comes to getting great food onto the table quickly. Personally, I never cut corners when it comes to flavour, but there are many tricks that I've learnt over the years for saving time while cooking. In this book, I share this knowledge and my experience to help you produce amazing meals fast. Every recipe can be cooked in roughly thirty minutes (we all move at different speeds, so there is a bit of give and take here), and, in my opinion, each one punches above its weight. What I mean by this is that the quality and tastiness of the finished dishes far outweigh the amount of effort put into cooking them. This is quick and easy food without compromising flavour in any way.

I know that modern life is busy and tiring, and that it's getting easier and easier to order a takeaway or have ready meals delivered to your home. But where's the satisfaction and pride in opening the door to a man in leathers and a helmet? And where's the pleasure and sense of achievement in pricking the cellophane of a ready meal before sticking it in the microwave? Cooking from scratch is better for you, much less expensive and so much more satisfying than buying dinner in. And it needn't take long to produce incredible food for yourself and your family. In fact, by the time your limp, sweaty takeaway has made it from the restaurant to your house, you could have made any of the knockout dishes in this book and be tucking into properly great food.

Producing restaurant-quality meals in half an hour can be a challenge. The time constraint rules out many of the techniques that chefs rely on to bring depth of flavour and complexity to a dish – marinating, braising, roasting and slow-cooking, for example. But there are ways around this if you know how: choose the right ingredients, marry them with the right combination of spices and sauces, use the right cooking method and you can produce incredibly tasty meals that tick all the boxes. Quick food doesn't mean bland and one-dimensional, especially when you bring in an arsenal of aromatic spices and condiments from across the globe (see pages 12–13). In fact, being short of time forces you to be more creative in the kitchen, not less.

When I'm at home, I don't want to spend hours cooking, but I still want to eat well. The recipes in this book are some of my go-to dishes when time is short but the appetite for something delicious is strong. Using bold flavours and some clever labour-saving cheats, I know I can produce top-quality food in under thirty minutes. If you follow the tips and techniques in these pages, you too will become a faster and better cook with a bigger repertoire of no-nonsense dishes from around the world. And by being well prepared, choosy about your ingredients and more efficient in the kitchen, you will be able to produce incredible food in no time at all. Shouldn't you be cooking already?

Gordan x

My Advice for Faster, Better Cooking

Clear the decks

The state of your kitchen before you start cooking will make a big difference to how you cook. Starting with a clean work surface, a sink clear of washing up and an empty dishwasher will help everything run more smoothly. A tidy kitchen leads to much better efficiency and, therefore, better food.

Switch off distractions

There's a reason that my chefs aren't allowed to use their mobile phones during service... Producing an amazing dish in a short space of time requires concentration and focus. I know that life can get in the way, but your cooking will be more successful if you give it your full attention.

Read the recipe before you start

I'm sure you've heard this piece of advice before, but how often do you actually follow it? It might seem like a waste of time when you're keen to get food on the table, but I can't emphasise enough how much time you will save if you do this. You will know exactly what to expect, what you need to prep in advance, and which pieces of kit you will need and when. Nothing is more frustrating than hunting for a whisk when you're halfway through a recipe.

Get your kit out

Before you start, know that you can easily lay your hands on all the kitchen equipment you need to complete the recipe. Get your scales/food processor/blender/mandolin out of the drawer or cupboard so you won't waste valuable minutes trying to find them. And sort out any jobs, such as lining a baking tray or setting up a bain-marie, at the outset. It will allow for a much smoother, stress-free process.

Get your mise-en-place in place

Getting all the ingredients ready before you begin will also save time once you start. Weigh out the things that need weighing, and gather all the spices, sauces and seasonings that you'll need. Reading the recipe through before you start means that you'll know what prep you will need to do upfront, and what you can leave for a suitable time in the process. For example, all the ingredients for a stir-fry need to be ready before you start, whereas the garnish for a soup can be prepped while the soup is cooking.

Buy the best

Professional chefs know that the secret to good cooking is actually good shopping. If you buy great ingredients, whether that's organic, well-aged meat, fruit and veg in the right season, or super-fresh seafood from a fishmonger, you are more than halfway there before you even start cooking. This is especially important when it comes to producing meals in a short space of time – the tastier the produce, the less you have to do to them to make them sing.

Take short cuts

When time is short, I'm all for cutting a few corners, such as buying ready-chopped butternut squash from a supermarket, or using pre-cooked rice. We don't think twice about buying tinned tomatoes, pre-cooked pulses, or jars of roasted peppers and artichokes, so why not use other unadulterated ingredients that have been prepped or cooked for you? I draw the line at shop-bought sauces and flavourless stock cubes, but if the ingredients haven't been messed about with in any way, feel free to save yourself a bit of time – especially if it means you are more likely to cook from scratch rather than resort to ready meals or a takeaway.

Clean up as you cook

It is good practice to tidy up as you go along. Keep a waste bowl next to your chopping board for the rubbish you create as you prep fruit and veg; that way you only need to make one trip to the bin at the end, rather than several time-wasting trips throughout. It keeps the work surface clear too. Chefs always wipe down their stations between tasks, and it's great to get into this habit. Fill a sink or washing-up bowl with warm soapy water so you can immediately put dirty pans and spoons in it (never put sharp knives in as they can cause accidents). Also, load the dishwasher as you go along. By the time you finish cooking, the washing up will virtually be done and it won't feel like a bomb has exploded in the kitchen.

Sharpen your knives

It is essential that your kitchen kit is in good condition. This is especially important when it comes to knives – a blunt knife is not only more dangerous, it is also seriously inefficient. Sharpen your knives before you start and every time you cook. It will make all the difference to prep times.

How to sharpen a knife

Hold the steel confidently in your non-dominant hand and use your other hand to place the heel of the knife (where the blade meets the handle) on top of the steel near its own handle. Draw the knife along the steel in a sweeping motion so that you stroke the entire length of the blade against it, keeping the angle between the steel and the blade at a steady 20 degrees. Now hone the other side of the knife by placing the blade under the steel and repeating the motion. Do this five or six times, alternating the side of the blade with each stroke, until you have a sharp edge. The more you do this, the quicker you will become.

Practise your knife skills

Chefs don't just hone their knife skills so they can look good chopping at speed on TV. They become good at wielding that knife so they can chop 5kg of onions in half the time it would take anyone else. Learn to use your knives like a professional and you too will speed through your veg, meat and fish prep. Go on a course or watch online tutorials, then practise what you've learnt every time you chop anything. Using your knife confidently and ergonomically will make you a faster, more effective cook.

Harness the heat

When you're trying to cook something quickly, it can be tempting to get it into the oven straight away, but if the oven hasn't had a chance to get up to the right temperature, it will take longer to cook and it will be more difficult to work out when to take it out again. Likewise, if you don't wait for a griddle pan to be smoking hot before you add your chops, it will take much more time to get a good colour on the outside of the meat, by which time the inside will be overcooked. Always wait for the oven to come up to temperature, for frying pans to be hot enough and for water to be actually boiling before you add any pasta or vegetables. Your food will thank you for it.

Kit List

Good cooking isn't dependent on having a kitchen full of gadgets. There are, however, a few pieces of equipment that will really help you to get delicious food onto the table in less time. Here is my list of essentials, starting with the most important.

Good knives

You can do almost everything with just three knives – a large chef's knife, a small paring knife and a serrated bread knife. Keep them sharp (see page 9), store them well (i.e. in a knife block or on a rack rather than loose in a drawer), and always wash them by hand. Follow these rules and your knives should last for years.

Blowtorch

Blowtorches aren't just for browning the sugar on top of a crème brûlée. We use them all the time in my kitchens to char the marinade on meat or fish, to melt cheesy toppings, and to caramelise sugar on all sorts of puddings. They take seconds to use and should be part of any speedy cook's arsenal.

Digital scales

Not only are they more accurate than old-fashioned kitchen scales, digital scales are also much faster to use. You can weigh all the ingredients straight into the measuring bowl, using the tare function to return the display to zero between each one. They're great for weighing liquids too.

Food processor

A food processor makes light work of jobs such as shredding cabbage or celeriac, grating cheese, puréeing soup and making fresh breadcrumbs. Use the smaller bowls for blitzing small amounts and whipping up dressings, marinades and sauces.

Grater

Whether you favour a good old-fashioned box grater or a fancy microplane, some sort of grater is essential for quickly grating a little bit of cheese, mincing a piece of ginger or zesting a lemon.

Mandolin

However good you are with a knife, a mandolin is incredibly useful for fast, uniform slicing. I use one repeatedly in this book because it is such an efficient way to slice beetroot, carrots, cucumber, apples and suchlike without having to get the food processor out.

Pestle and mortar

A large, heavy pestle and mortar is a great piece of kitchen kit for pounding and grinding herbs and spices, unleashing their flavour without totally pulverising them.

Speedy peeler

The clue is in the name – a swivel peeler will make light work of peeling fruit and veg, and as it removes only the skin or outermost layer, you are left with more of the flesh. It's also great for shaving hard cheeses, and for quickly slicing veg into ribbons.

Stick blender

A stick blender is so useful for quickly blitzing hot soups, dips and dressings on the spot. You can also use it for making smoothies, bringing batters together and whipping cream.

Silicone baking mat

Lining a baking tray with a silicone mat takes literally seconds and there are no burning issues as with baking paper. You can also use them over and over again, which is much better for the environment than tin foil and baking paper.

Shortcuts to Flavour

When time is short, seasoning is vital as there isn't time to develop the deep flavours associated with roasting, braising and slow cooking. It's therefore important to keep a well-stocked store cupboard. Having an array of different sauces and spices will mean you are never far away from a quick, tasty meal. I am assuming that you have olive oil, some sort of vegetable or sunflower oil for frying, some vinegars, mustard and salt and pepper, as well as a collection of herbs and spices, but here is a list of ingredients you might not already have, which are guaranteed to liven things up.

Dashi powder

Dashi is Japanese stock made from the seaweed kombu, which is rich in umami and forms the base of many Japanese dishes, from miso soup to ramen noodle broths. Powdered dashi is the quickest way to inject that savoury richness into your cooking.

Fennel pollen

An intense, aniseed-flavoured spice from the flowers of the fennel plant, this is great sprinkled over fish, chicken, pork and salads.

Fish sauce

A stalwart of East and South-east Asian cooking, fish sauce is a fermented condiment that brings a savoury umami hit to dipping sauces, noodles, soups and stir-fries.

Furikake seasoning

A tasty mixture that typically contains black and white sesame seeds, dried seaweed and dried fish. The Japanese use it mostly for sprinkling over rice; it can also be used to instantly pep up fish, chicken and rice dishes.

Gochujang chilli paste

Fermented chilli paste from Korea that is sweet, savoury and very hot all at the same time. Brilliant in marinades and sauces, it can also be stirred through stews, stir-fries and soups.

Harissa

A fragrant chilli and red pepper paste from North Africa that is used to flavour meat, couscous, stews and sauces. Rose harissa is a fragrant variation in which the rose petals temper the chilli and add a gentle sweetness.

Lemongrass paste

All the fragrant intensity of fresh lemongrass in a very useful paste.

Mirin

A sweetened rice wine from Japan that is a bit like saké. It is used to add a sweet tang to dipping sauces, broths and marinades.

Miso paste

Japanese fermented soya bean paste that is packed with umami. It can be white, yellow, red, or simply dark, depending on how long it has been fermented, with white being the mildest and red being saltier and stronger.

Paprika

Can be hot, sweet, smoked or unsmoked, but whichever type you use, paprika will add an instant smokiness and depth to your food.

Ras-el-hanout

A Moroccan spice mix that instantly transports you to the souks of North Africa, this is an easy way to add an exotic taste to rubs, marinades and tagines.

Time-saving Ingredients

Rice vinegar

A mild, slightly sweet vinegar used to bring a subtle acidity to sauces, marinades and stir-fries.

Saffron

The mild spice that brings a golden yellow colour and subtle but distinct aroma and flavour to sauces, risottos, pasta, fish and chicken dishes.

Shaoxing rice wine

A fermented rice wine that gives depth and complexity to Chinese sauces and soups.

Shichimi togarashi (seven-spice powder)

A tasty blend of seven spices, including chilli flakes, orange peel, sesame seeds and ground ginger; it is used to brighten up soups, noodle dishes, grilled meat and fish.

Sichuan peppercorns

A lip-tingling pepper-like spice that adds a fragrant punch to Chinese cooking.

Sriracha sauce

Thailand's versatile chilli sauce, which is hot and tangy with a gentle sweetness.

Sumac

A citrusy spice popular across North Africa; it can be sprinkled over dishes to add the sharpness of lemons and limes.

Tamarind paste

Adds an instant sweet-and-sour note to sauces and marinades.

Thai shrimp paste

A paste that imparts the strong salty paste of fermented shrimps, and adds body to South-east Asian curries and noodle soups.

It isn't cheating to buy ready-prepped ingredients – it's like having a secret sous chef in your cupboard and a commis chef in the freezer! But make sure that the ingredients you buy have just been chopped or cooked rather than adulterated in any way. Here's a list of things to buy to help speed up your cooking.

- Frozen chopped chillies, onions and herbs
- Frozen peas and spinach
- Pre-chopped veg, especially those that are tricky to peel, such as butternut squash and pumpkin
- Spiralised vegetables
- Cauliflower 'rice'
- Cooked beetroot
- Bags of salad leaves
- Tinned tomatoes, beans and pulses
- Roast peppers and artichokes
- Crispy fried onions
- Fresh pasta and noodles
- Pre-cooked rice
- Ready-made pastry (puff and shortcrust)
- Breadcrumbs, dry and fresh
- Fresh stock

Soups
and
Salads

Cauliflower Soup with Brown Butter and Cheesy Toasts 19

Chicken and Shiitake Noodle Soup 20

Celeriac and Apple Soup with Crushed Walnuts 23

Spiced Squash and Lentil Soup 24

Soba Noodle, Courgette and Brown Shrimp Salad with Tamari Dressing 27

Kale Caesar Salad with Garlic Croutons 28

Warm Aubergine, Tomato and Burrata 31

Halloumi, Asparagus and Green Bean Salad 32

Beetroot Salad with Whipped Goat's Cheese 35

Vietnamese Meatball Noodle Salad 36

Cauliflower Soup with Brown Butter and Cheesy Toasts

Serves 4

2 tbsp olive oil
20g butter
1 onion, peeled and finely chopped
2 garlic cloves, peeled and sliced
Small handful of sage leaves
1 x 800g cauliflower
500ml chicken or vegetable stock
200ml whole milk
200ml double cream
Sea salt and freshly ground pepper

For the brown butter
40g butter
1 tbsp truffle oil
Handful of sage leaves

For the cheesy toasts
4 slices of baguette, finely sliced
    on the diagonal
120g grated cheese mixture
    (mozzarella, Cheddar, blue and
    Gruyère, or a combination of
    whatever you have in the fridge)

Time-saving tip
If you warm the stock in a saucepan over a medium heat while you prep the onions, garlic and cauliflower, it will come to the boil quicker when you add it to the soup pan, therefore speeding up the whole process.

Making brown butter, or *buerre noisette*, is one of those techniques that chefs love but home cooks seem to steer clear of because it sounds tricky. Believe me, it's really not complicated, and the more often you do it, the more confident you become at judging the right time to take the pan off the heat. It's such an easy way to add a rich nuttiness to this creamy soup, and it smells incredible.

1 Preheat the grill.

2 Place a large saucepan over a medium heat and add the oil and butter. When the butter has melted, add the onion and garlic and cook for 5 minutes. Add the sage leaves and cook for a further minute.

3 Meanwhile, prepare the cauliflower by removing the leaves and separating the florets. Roughly chop them into small pieces of the same size.

4 Add the chopped cauliflower and the stock to the pan. Season with salt and pepper, bring to the boil and simmer for 5 minutes. Add the milk and cream, and simmer for a further 8 minutes.

5 Meanwhile, make the brown butter. Put the butter into a small saucepan and place it over a high heat. When it begins to brown, remove the pan from the heat and add the truffle oil and sage leaves. Stir well and leave to cool.

6 Now make the toasts. Lay the baguette slices on a baking tray and grill for 2–3 minutes, or until lightly golden on one side. Turn each slice over, then sprinkle liberally with the grated cheese. Replace under the grill for a further 4 minutes, or until the cheese is melted and golden.

7 When the cauliflower is cooked, blend the mixture with a stick blender until smooth. Check the seasoning and adjust as necessary. Ladle the soup into bowls and spoon over the brown butter and sage leaves. Serve with the cheesy toasts on the side.

Chicken and Shiitake Noodle Soup

Serves 4

1.5 litres chicken stock
4 chicken thighs, skin on
12 dried shiitake mushrooms
2–3cm piece of fresh root ginger,
    peeled and julienned
1 star anise
2 spring onions, trimmed and
    cut in half
100ml Shaoxing rice wine
180g egg noodles
2 tbsp soy sauce
200g choi sum
Sea salt and ground white pepper

To serve
80g bamboo shoots
Asian microherbs or coriander leaves
2 tsp sesame oil

Time-saving tip
Peel ginger with a teaspoon –
it takes less time than using
a knife and there is less waste.

I love the different broths and noodle soups you find across countries such as China, Japan, Malaysia and Vietnam. The broths for these soups are usually laboured over for many hours to give them an intense depth of flavour, but this soup uses dried shiitake mushrooms to shortcut the process. They are really rich in umami, bringing a wonderful savouriness and depth to the dish in no time at all.

1 Place a saucepan over a high heat. Pour in the chicken stock, then add the chicken thighs and mushrooms.
2 Add the ginger to the pan along with the star anise, spring onions and rice wine. Season with a big pinch of sea salt and a small pinch of white pepper.
3 Bring the soup to the boil, skimming off any impurities that might rise to the surface. Once boiling, reduce the heat to a strong simmer and cook for 10 minutes.
4 Meanwhile, bring a kettle of water to the boil. Pour into a clean saucepan over a high heat and season with salt. Add the noodles and cook for 3–4 minutes, or until just tender. Drain the noodles and hold them under running cold water until cool. Drain again and put to one side until needed.
5 Remove a chicken thigh from the broth and check if it is cooked through by piercing the thickest part with the tip of a sharp knife; the juices should run clear with no pinkness. If cooked, remove all the chicken pieces and the mushrooms from the broth and put to one side.
6 Using a slotted spoon, remove the star anise, ginger and spring onions from the broth and return it to a high heat. Add the soy sauce and taste for seasoning.
7 Roughly chop the choi sum into 7cm lengths, and separate the stalks from the leafy parts. Add the stalks to the saucepan and allow to cook for 2 minutes.
8 Remove the skin from the chicken thighs and shred the meat, discarding the bones.
9 Add the choi sum to the broth and turn the heat off.
10 Divide the noodles between four bowls and top with the shiitake mushrooms, chicken and choi sum then ladle over the broth. Garnish with the bamboo shoots and microherbs and a drizzle of sesame oil.

Celeriac and Apple Soup with Crushed Walnuts

Serves 4–6

1 onion, peeled and roughly chopped

1 celeriac (600–800g), peeled
and diced

2 Cox's apples, peeled, cored
and roughly chopped

2 tbsp olive oil

1 tbsp thyme leaves

1 litre vegetable stock

Sea salt and freshly ground black
or white pepper

To serve

Large handful of walnuts, roughly
chopped

Extra virgin olive oil, for drizzling

Celeriac makes the most delicious creamy soup even without adding any cream or milk (great for vegans), but it can be very rich on its own. Adding sweet but sharp apples, such as Cox's, cuts through the richness and complements the flavour beautifully. I also love the contrast between the smooth, creamy texture of the soup and the crunchy walnuts.

1 Prepare the onion, celeriac and apples as listed.

2 Place a large saucepan over a medium heat and add the olive oil. When hot, add the onion with a pinch of salt and cook for 4–5 minutes, or until soft but not coloured.

3 Add the celeriac, apples and thyme leaves and cook for 5 minutes.

4 Pour in the vegetable stock and bring to a simmer. Continue simmering for 5 more minutes, or until the celeriac is tender.

5 Remove the pan from the heat and use a stick blender to blend thoroughly. Season with salt and pepper, then taste and add more seasoning as necessary.

6 Ladle into warm bowls, scatter with the chopped walnuts and drizzle with some extra virgin olive oil before serving.

Spiced Squash and Lentil Soup

Serves 4

1 tbsp light olive oil
40g butter
1 onion, peeled and diced
1 tsp cumin seeds
4 garlic cloves, peeled
5cm piece of fresh root ginger,
    peeled
2 red chillies, deseeded if you want
    a milder hit
1 tsp mild curry powder
1kg butternut squash
1.2 litres chicken or vegetable stock
250g red lentils
250ml coconut cream
Sea salt and freshly ground black
    pepper

To garnish

2 tbsp light olive oil
1 tsp cumin seeds
Large handful of fresh curry leaves
½ tsp mild curry powder
1 red chilli, deseeded if you want
    a milder hit, finely sliced

Time-saving tip

For a really quick and easy way to peel lots of garlic cloves, put them into a metal saucepan with a tight-fitting lid and shake the pan really vigorously with both hands for about 30 seconds, or until all the garlic cloves are miraculously peeled. This also works for a whole bulb!

Soup is the ultimate fast food, and this hearty meal-in-a-bowl is a great example – it is nourishing, warming and filling, and takes only half an hour to rustle up. I usually make a double batch and freeze it for an even quicker meal down the line. Suddenly winter evenings don't seem so dark and cold! Use vegetable stock to make this soup vegan.

1 Heat the oil and butter in a large saucepan over a medium heat. When the butter has melted, add the onion and cumin seeds and cook for 2–3 minutes.

2 Meanwhile, place the garlic, ginger and chillies in a small food processor and blend to a paste. Add this to the pan along with the curry powder and cook for another 2–3 minutes.

3 Prepare the squash by peeling the skin off and removing all the seeds with a spoon. Cut the flesh into 1cm cubes and add to the pan together with the stock. Increase the heat to high and bring to the boil.

4 Add the lentils and cook for 10 minutes.

5 Put the coconut cream into a small bowl and whisk until smooth. Reserve 6 tablespoons for the garnish and add the rest to the pan. Cook over a high heat, until the pumpkin is soft and the lentils are cooked.

6 While the soup is cooking, heat the oil for the garnish in a small frying pan. When hot, add the cumin seeds, curry leaves and curry powder. Stir well, then remove the pan from the heat.

7 Using a stick blender, blend the soup until smooth, then season with salt and pepper and ladle into individual bowls. Drizzle over the reserved coconut cream and the curry oil. Sprinkle with a few slices of red chilli before serving.

Soba Noodle, Courgette and Brown Shrimp Salad with Tamari Dressing

Serves 4

200g soba noodles
Groundnut oil, for drizzling
200g spiralised 'courgetti'
  (about 2 courgettes)
150g cooked brown shrimps
150g cherry tomatoes, halved
25g chives, finely chopped
2 tbsp sesame seeds

For the tamari dressing
½ tsp Dijon mustard
1½ tbsp rice vinegar
1 tbsp sesame oil
2 tbsp tamari soy sauce
1 tbsp mirin
50ml olive oil
2cm piece of fresh root ginger,
  peeled and grated
1 garlic clove, peeled and crushed
Pinch of sea salt

This Japanese-inspired noodle salad is packed full of flavour and bite. You can spiralise your own courgettes if you have a spiraliser and time on your hands, but these days you can buy 'courgetti' from some supermarkets. Alternatively, use a mandolin or julienne grater to shred the courgettes before adding them to the noodles. Be wary of adding too much salt to the dressing as soba noodles and tamari soy sauce contain plenty already.

1 Bring a kettle of water to the boil, then pour it into a large saucepan. Return to the boil over a medium–high heat, then add the soba noodles and cook for 4 minutes. Drain and rinse under cold water to cool the noodles quickly. Drain thoroughly, then drizzle with a little groundnut oil to stop the noodles sticking together.

2 Put the cooled noodles into a large bowl and add the spiralised courgette, the shrimps, tomatoes and chives.

3 To make the dressing, put all the ingredients into a bowl and whisk to combine.

4 Toast the sesame seeds in a dry frying pan for 2–3 minutes, or until golden, shaking the pan regularly.

5 Pour the dressing over the salad and toss well to ensure that all the ingredients are well coated. Scatter over the toasted sesame seeds before serving.

Kale Caesar Salad with Garlic Croutons

Serves 4

1 large garlic clove, peeled and
   crushed
3 tbsp olive oil
2 tbsp flat leaf parsley, finely
   chopped
150g sourdough bread
1 tbsp vegetable oil
200g smoked bacon lardons
100g mixed kale (green and purple,
   if available)
4 little gem lettuces
100g baby chestnut mushrooms,
   finely sliced
½ red onion, peeled and finely sliced
8 anchovies in olive oil
40g Parmesan cheese
Sea salt and freshly ground black
   pepper

For the dressing

100g good-quality French
   mayonnaise
1 large garlic clove, peeled and
   crushed
20g Parmesan cheese, finely grated
1 tsp Dijon mustard
Juice of ½ lemon
8 anchovies in olive oil (optional)
1–2 tbsp water

You can't escape kale these days: it crops up in scrambled eggs, smoothies, pasta sauces, on pizzas, even in cakes and brownies – pretty good for a once deeply unfashionable type of cabbage! Tana and I have embraced these dark leafy greens in our house as she loves kale and tries to sneak it into the kids at every opportunity. I, on the other hand, think it makes a great addition to a classic Caesar salad, but don't let it anywhere near my brownies!

1   Preheat the oven to 220°C/200°C fan/Gas 7. Line a baking tray with baking paper.

2   Put the garlic, olive oil and parsley into a bowl, season with salt and pepper and mix well.

3   Tear the sourdough into small pieces and put them into the bowl with the garlic oil. Mix until well coated, then spread the bread over the prepared tray. Place in the oven and cook for 8–10 minutes, or until golden brown.

4   Place a large non-stick frying pan over a medium–high heat. When hot, add the vegetable oil, then the lardons and cook for 5–8 minutes, or until crispy.

5   Meanwhile, make the dressing: put the mayonnaise, garlic, Parmesan, mustard and lemon juice into a bowl. Chop the anchovies, add to the bowl and stir to combine. Add the water to loosen the dressing.

6   Tear the kale into bite-sized pieces. Trim the lettuces and separate the leaves. Cut the larger leaves in half lengthways and keep the smaller leaves whole. Put all the leaves into a salad bowl with the sliced mushrooms and red onion.

7   Pour the dressing over the salad and toss well. Scatter over the croutons and bacon lardons, then cut the remaining anchovies in half lengthways and lay them on top (if using). Using a vegetable peeler, shave the Parmesan over the salad before serving.

Warm Aubergine, Tomato and Burrata

Serves 4

3 aubergines, trimmed and sliced
   1cm thick
4 tbsp olive oil
850g heritage tomatoes, sliced
   1cm thick
80g rocket leaves
3 burratas
Sea salt

For the dressing
60ml olive oil
1 banana shallot, peeled and finely
   diced
2 garlic cloves, peeled and finely
   diced
3 rosemary sprigs, leaves picked and
   finely chopped
40ml red wine vinegar
½ tsp chilli flakes (optional)
Freshly ground black pepper

I know chefs are always banging on about how much the quality of the ingredients matters, but it's absolutely true that if you source the best produce, more than half the work is already done before you even get into the kitchen. That truth is never more apparent than when it comes to an uncomplicated salad like this one... there is nowhere to hide. Make sure you use sweet, ripe tomatoes and firm aubergines in season, then splash out on really good-quality, creamy burrata and you can't go wrong.

1 Place a griddle pan over a high heat.
2 Brush each aubergine slice with a little of the olive oil and sprinkle with salt. Lay a few of the slices, oil side down, on the griddle, brush the tops with a little more oil and sprinkle with a little more salt. Cook for 2–3 minutes on each side, or until charred and soft. Repeat with the remaining slices.
3 Pour the oil for the dressing into a small saucepan and place over a medium heat for 2–3 minutes. It is hot enough when a piece of shallot addcd to the pan sizzles gently. Turn the heat off, then add all the shallot, the garlic and rosemary and mix well. Leave to cook gently for 2–3 minutes, then add the vinegar and chilli flakes (if using) and season with salt and pepper.
4 Layer the aubergine slices and tomatoes in a shallow bowl or on a platter. Drizzle each layer with a little of the dressing, then sprinkle with the rocket. Cut each burrata in half and place on top. Drizzle with the remaining dressing and serve.

Halloumi, Asparagus and Green Bean Salad

Serves 2

250g fine green beans, trimmed
100g fine asparagus, trimmed
250g halloumi cheese
½ tsp chilli flakes
1 tbsp olive oil
200g cherry tomatoes, halved
50g pitted Kalamata olives
Small handful of pea shoots
Sea salt and freshly ground black
   pepper

For the dressing
2 basil sprigs, leaves picked
2 mint sprigs, leaves picked
1 tbsp red wine vinegar
3 tbsp extra virgin olive oil

Time-saving tip
To trim beans in no time at all,
line them up in the bag so that
all the woody ends are together,
then use a chef's knife to cut
through the plastic and trim all
the beans in one go.

You can keep unopened halloumi for up to a year in the fridge, so you are never more than half an hour away from a cracking summer lunch like this one. I love the combination of asparagus, green beans, tomatoes and olives, but you can replace these, or add to them, with whatever you have in the fridge on the day: avocado, cucumber, edamame beans, mixed salad leaves and griddled courgettes all work well.

1 Bring a kettle of water to the boil, then pour it into a saucepan. Season with salt and place it over a high heat. Once boiling again, add the beans and cook for 4 minutes, then add the asparagus and cook for a further minute. Drain and place the vegetables in a large bowl of iced water to stop the cooking process.

2 To make the dressing, put the basil and mint leaves into a small food processor with the vinegar and oil. Season with salt and pepper and blend until smooth.

3 Cut the halloumi in half horizontally so you have two rectangles. Sprinkle each one with some of the chilli flakes.

4 Place a non-stick frying pan over a medium–high heat. When hot, add the oil and gently swirl it to coat the base evenly. Put the halloumi slices into the pan, chilli side down, and sprinkle the top with a little more chilli. Cook for 2–3 minutes on each side, or until golden brown.

5 Meanwhile, drain the beans and asparagus and put into a bowl with the cherry tomatoes and half the dressing. Mix well and divide between two plates. Place the halloumi on top.

6 Add the olives to the frying pan to warm through, then sprinkle them around the halloumi. Drizzle with the remaining dressing and garnish with a few pea shoots before serving.

Beetroot Salad with Whipped Goat's Cheese

Serves 2

40g hazelnuts
1 raw candy beetroot
4 cooked beetroots (about 250g
  in total)
½ bag (60g) shop-bought beetroot
  salad mixture

For the dressing

1 tbsp sherry vinegar
1 tbsp beetroot juice (optional)
1 tsp Dijon mustard
3 tbsp extra virgin olive oil
Sea salt and freshly ground black
  pepper

For the whipped cheese

100g soft goat's cheese
50g cream cheese
Zest of ½ lemon
2 lemon thyme sprigs, leaves picked
1–2 tsp water

Time-saving tip

There's no need to peel the
beetroot if you use a cookie
cutter to stamp circles out of
the slices. Apart from saving
time, you get uniform shapes
that look really smart and
professional. This technique
also works for sliced apples,
potatoes and other root veg.

If you can get hold of a striped candy beetroot,
it transforms this salad from a nice-looking dish
to a stunning one. The combination of the cooked
and raw beetroots provides texture and crunch, and
maximises both the sweet and earthy flavours of the
beets. A mandolin makes light work of the slicing, but
if you don't have one, use a very sharp chef's knife
and slice the beetroot as finely as you can.

1 Preheat the oven to 200°C/180°C fan/Gas 4.
2 Spread the hazelnuts over a small baking tray and
  place in the oven for 5–8 minutes, or until they turn
  a dark golden brown.
3 Meanwhile, put all the dressing ingredients into a small
  bowl. Season with salt and pepper and whisk well.
4 Using a mandolin or sharp knife, slice the candy
  beetroot very finely, then use a round pastry cutter
  (about 6.5cm in diameter) to stamp a circle from each
  slice. Place the circles in the dressing to pickle lightly.
5 Remove the hazelnuts from the oven and leave to cool.
6 Place the whipped cheese ingredients in a food
  processor with a pinch of salt and pepper. Blend
  until smooth, adding a little more water to loosen
  if necessary. Place in the fridge until needed.
7 Quarter the cooked beetroots and put them into
  a bowl with the salad mixture. Add half the dressing,
  season and mix well, then divide between two plates.
  Lift the slices of candy beetroot from the dressing and
  place on the salad. Dot with spoonfuls of the whipped
  goat's cheese and spoon over the remaining dressing.
8 Using the flat side of your knife, crush the hazelnuts
  on a chopping board so they are lightly broken up.
  Sprinkle some over each plate to serve.

Vietnamese Meatball Noodle Salad

Serves 2

250g minced pork
2 tsp lemongrass paste
1 tbsp fish sauce
1 tsp white sugar
1 garlic clove, peeled and crushed
2 spring onions, trimmed and finely
   chopped
Pinch of ground white pepper
1 tbsp vegetable oil

For the salad
100g rice vermicelli noodles
1 large carrot, peeled and julienned
½ cucumber, julienned
2 handfuls of beansprouts
8 little gem lettuce leaves
Fresh mint and coriander leaves
20g salted peanuts, roughly
   chopped

For the dressing
30ml fish sauce
30ml rice vinegar
1 tbsp caster sugar
Juice of ½ lime
1 garlic clove, peeled and finely
   chopped
30ml water
½ red chilli, deseeded if you want
   a milder hit, finely chopped

Time-saving tip
Wetting your hands before rolling
the meatballs will stop the meat
from sticking to your fingers,
but coating your hands in a thin
layer of vegetable oil is even more
effective and you won't have to
keep wetting and re-wetting them.

The Vietnamese have really mastered the art of packing lots of vibrant flavours and crisp textures into one bowl. This salad has the crunch of carrots, cucumber, beansprouts and peanuts, plus the zing of mint, chilli and lemongrass, while the dressing has the bite of fish sauce and rice vinegar. It covers all the bases and is extremely satisfying as a result.

1 Put the pork, lemongrass paste, fish sauce, white sugar, crushed garlic, spring onions and white pepper into a bowl and mix well with clean hands. Divide into 12 equal pieces, then roll each one into a ball and flatten slightly. Put to one side.

2 Bring a kettle of water to the boil. Put the noodles into a large, heatproof bowl and pour over enough boiling water to cover them. Put to one side for 10 minutes.

3 Meanwhile, prepare the carrot and cucumber.

4 When the noodles are soft, drain them and hold under cold running water until cool. Drain again and put them to one side until needed.

5 Place a large non-stick frying pan over a medium–high heat and add the vegetable oil. When hot, add the meatballs and cook for 2–3 minutes on each side, or until golden brown and cooked through.

6 While the meatballs are cooking, put all the dressing ingredients in a bowl and mix well.

7 Divide the noodles between two serving bowls and add the carrot, cucumber, beansprouts, lettuce leaves and fresh herbs. Top with the cooked meatballs. Spoon some of the dressing over the salad and serve the rest on the side. Scatter over the peanuts before serving.

Fish
and
Shellfish

Fish Finger Sandwiches 43

Pan-fried Salmon with Pink Grapefruit Hollandaise 44

Moules Marinière with Wild Garlic Toasts 47

Baked Halibut with Borlotti Beans and Tomatoes 48

Scallops with Creamed Corn and Pancetta 51

Squid and Fennel Stew 52

Miso-glazed Cod 55

Grilled Mackerel with Orange Gremolata Dressing 56

Malaysian Fish and Okra Curry 59

Tuna Steaks with Preserved Lemon Couscous 60

Baked Sea Bream with Fennel, Carrot and Lemon 63

Garlic and Chilli Prawns 64

Pan-fried Salmon with Warm Potato Salad 67

Chinese-style Baked Sea Bass 68

Salt and Pink Pepper Prawns with Lime Mayonnaise 71

Roast Hake with Saffron Mayonnaise 72

Fish Finger Sandwiches

Serves 2

300g haddock or cod fillets
4 tbsp plain flour
1 egg
1 tbsp whole milk
50g panko breadcrumbs
1 tbsp chopped dill
2 ciabatta or brioche rolls
Vegetable oil, for frying
Large handful of watercress
Sea salt and freshly ground
   black pepper

For the tartare sauce

4 tbsp good-quality French
   mayonnaise
1 shallot, peeled and finely diced
4 cornichons, finely chopped
2 tsp nonpareille capers
1 tbsp finely chopped flat leaf parsley
Lemon juice, to taste

Chef's tip

Before coating the fish in the panko, rub the breadcrumbs through your fingers to make sure they are all the same size – they will cook much more evenly.

What I really want to achieve in this book is to show you how quick and satisfying producing food from scratch can be and how much more delicious it is than a ready meal. This fish finger sandwich is a case in point. Yes, you could bung some frozen fish fingers in the oven and open a jar of shop-bought tartare sauce, but it wouldn't taste even half as amazing as this fish finger butty. Try it and you'll see what I mean.

1   Cut the fish into 4 equal 'fingers' and season both sides with salt and pepper.

2   Set out three shallow bowls. Put the flour into one and season with salt and pepper too. Put the egg and milk into another bowl and lightly beat together. Put the breadcrumbs and dill into a third bowl and mix well.

3   Dust the fish in the flour, shake off any excess, then dip into the egg mixture, making sure all the sides are coated. Finally, cover in the breadcrumbs. Transfer to a plate and place the fish fingers in the fridge.

4   Preheat the grill to medium–high.

5   Make the tartare sauce by mixing all the ingredients together with a little salt and pepper.

6   Cut the rolls in half and put them on a tray, cut side up. Place under the grill for 1–2 minutes, or until golden and toasted.

7   Place a frying pan over a medium–high heat and add a 1cm depth of vegetable oil. When hot, shallow-fry the fish fingers for 2–3 minutes on each side, or until crisp and golden all over. Remove from the oil and drain on kitchen paper, then season each one with a little salt.

8   Spread the tartare sauce on the bottom half of each bun. Put the fish fingers on the tartare sauce, then top with the watercress before putting the lids on to serve.

Pan-fried Salmon with Pink Grapefruit Hollandaise

Serves 4

4 x 200g salmon fillets,
   skin on and pin-boned
1 tbsp mild olive oil
450g asparagus, trimmed
100ml water
25g butter
1 tsp pink peppercorns
Pink grapefruit wedges, to serve
   (optional)

For the pink grapefruit hollandaise
50ml dry white wine
80ml white wine vinegar
1 small shallot, peeled and finely
   chopped
2 tarragon sprigs, roughly chopped
200g butter
2 egg yolks
1 tbsp pink grapefruit juice
1 tsp pink grapefruit zest
1 tbsp finely sliced chives
Sea salt and finely ground black
   pepper

I know hollandaise sauce has a reputation for being tricky to make, but if you take your time when you add the butter and don't let it get too hot, you can produce an amazing, restaurant-quality sauce in your own kitchen. The tart grapefruit cuts through the buttery richness of the sauce and gives it a very slight pink blush that looks stunning with the salmon and pink peppercorns.

1 Start by making the hollandaise sauce: put the wine, vinegar, shallot and tarragon into a small saucepan and heat until reduced to about 2 tablespoons of liquid. Strain, discarding the solids, and set aside until needed.

2 Melt the 200g butter over a gentle heat and carefully pour the golden liquid into a jug, discarding the milky solids at the bottom of the pan.

3 Place a heatproof bowl over a pan of simmering water. Add the egg yolks, grapefruit juice and zest plus half of the reduced vinegar. Whisk until frothy and thick, then slowly add the melted butter, whisking constantly. Stir through the chives, then season with salt and pepper and add a little warm water if it's too thick. Add the remaining vinegar reduction if you prefer a bit more tang. Put to one side.

4 Score the skin on the salmon fillets, then brush with the olive oil and season on both sides with salt and pepper. Place a large, non-stick frying pan over a medium–high heat and, when hot, add the salmon, skin side down. Reduce the heat to medium–low and cook for about 5 minutes, until the skin is quite crisp. Flip over and cook the other side for 2–3 minutes, until slightly springy to the touch. Remove and allow the fish to rest for a few minutes.

5 Meanwhile, put the asparagus into a large sauté pan with the water, butter and a little salt and pepper. Place over a high heat and cook for 5 minutes, or until tender.

6 Put a salmon fillet on each serving plate and place some asparagus alongside. Spoon the hollandaise over the salmon and sprinkle with a few pink peppercorns. If you wish, serve with a wedge of pink grapefruit on the side.

Moules Marinière with Wild Garlic Toasts

Serves 2

1kg mussels
2 tbsp olive oil
2 banana shallots, peeled and finely
 diced
1 large garlic clove, peeled and finely
 chopped
125ml dry white wine, e.g. Muscadet
150ml double cream
Large handful of wild garlic leaves,
 finely chopped
30g butter

For the wild garlic toasts
150g butter, softened
Handful of wild garlic, roughly
 chopped
4–6 slices of baguette, sliced on
 the diagonal
20g Parmesan cheese
Sea salt and freshly ground black
 pepper

Chef's tip
If you have more wild garlic than
you need, make double the butter
recipe, roll it into a log and freeze
it for future use. It's delicious
melted onto a steak or stirred
through risotto, and can be
used to make the Wild Garlic
Turkey Kievs on page 87.

Mussels are one of my favourite shellfish – they are cheap, healthy and delicious, need minimal prep and you can cook them in minutes. This version of the classic French dish uses the subtle wild garlic leaves that can be foraged in woodlands from March to May, or found at farmers' markets or from specialist suppliers. If you can't get your hands on wild garlic, double the amount of regular garlic in the liquor and add a crushed clove to the butter for the toasts.

1   Preheat the grill to medium–high.
2   Wash and debeard the mussels, then drain in a colander.
3   Place a large casserole dish that has a tight-fitting lid over a medium heat and add the oil. When hot, add the shallots and cook for 2–3 minutes, or until softened. Stir in the garlic and cook for 1 minute, then add the wine. Simmer until the wine reduces by half.
4   Meanwhile, to make the wild garlic butter for the toasts, put the 150g butter into a small food processor with the roughly chopped wild garlic and a little salt and pepper. Blend until well combined. Set aside.
5   Add the cream and finely chopped wild garlic to the wine mixture, increase the heat to high and let it reduce by half.
6   Meanwhile, put the baguette slices on a baking tray and place under the grill for 2 minutes, or until golden and toasted on one side. Remove from the grill, flip each slice over, then spread thickly with the wild garlic butter. Using a fine grater, grate the Parmesan directly over each slice of baguette until evenly coated, then grill for 2 more minutes, or until golden brown.
7   Add the mussels to the wine pan and stir well. Put the lid on and cook for 4–5 minutes, or until all the mussels have opened. Discard any that haven't opened, then stir the 30g butter into the sauce and serve immediately with the wild garlic toasts.

Baked Halibut with Borlotti Beans and Tomatoes

Serves 4

450g baby plum tomatoes
2 x 400g tins of borlotti beans, drained and rinsed
4 x 200g halibut fillets, skinned
Pinch of chilli flakes
2 garlic cloves, peeled and finely sliced
1 tbsp nonpareille capers
2 rosemary sprigs, leaves finely chopped
1 unwaxed lemon, finely sliced
150ml dry white wine
3 tbsp olive oil
350g purple sprouting broccoli
100ml water
30g butter
Sea salt and freshly ground black pepper
Small handful of basil leaves, to serve (optional)

You can't beat an all-in-one traybake for ease and speed, and a meaty fish like halibut is perfect for the job. The tomatoes and wine will ensure the fish doesn't dry out while cooking, and everything in the tray will absorb all the lovely flavours of the lemon, rosemary and garlic, making this a super-tasty midweek supper that will go down a storm with all the family.

1 Preheat the oven to 220°C/200°C fan/Gas 7.
2 Put the tomatoes and borlotti beans into a roasting tray and season with a little salt and pepper.
3 Season both sides of the fish with salt and pepper and place them on top of the beans and tomatoes. Sprinkle the fish with chilli flakes, then scatter the garlic, capers and rosemary over everything in the tray. Put the lemon slices on top, then pour over the wine and drizzle with olive oil.
4 Place the tray on the top shelf of the oven for 12–15 minutes, or until the fish is cooked through.
5 Meanwhile, place the broccoli in a large sauté pan with the water and butter. Season with salt and pepper and cook for 5 minutes, turning halfway through for even cooking.
6 When the halibut is cooked, sprinkle with the basil leaves and serve with the broccoli and crusty bread.

Scallops with Creamed Corn and Pancetta

Serves 2

200g fine green beans, trimmed
1 tbsp olive oil
8–10 scallops, with roe attached
1 tbsp butter
Sea salt and freshly ground black
    pepper

For the creamed corn

80g pancetta, finely diced
1 tbsp olive oil
1 onion, peeled and finely diced
2 corn on the cob
2 garlic cloves, peeled and finely
    chopped
½ tsp paprika
200ml double cream
2 thyme sprigs, leaves picked
100ml water
2 tbsp freshly grated Parmesan
    cheese
50g sour cream
2 tbsp flat leaf parsley

Time-saving tip

If you are really in a hurry, use
tinned unsweetened corn instead
of fresh corn kernels and reduce
the cooking time by 5 minutes.

Corn, bacon and scallops make an incredible combination – sweet, salty and extremely satisfying. The scallops cook very fast, so wait until the last minute before cooking them. I always add them to the edge of the pan in a clockwise direction, starting at 12 o'clock, so by the time you have put them all into the pan, it's time to turn the first ones that went in. It's a simple technique for ensuring that all the scallops cook evenly.

1   Start by making the creamed corn. Place a small, non-stick frying pan over a medium heat. When hot, add the pancetta and cook for 2–3 minutes, or until the fat begins to render.
2   Meanwhile, place a saucepan over a medium–high heat and add the oil. When hot, add the onion and cook for 5 minutes, or until softened.
3   Remove the corn kernels from the cobs by standing each cob upright and running a sharp knife down the sides. Add a handful of the corn to the pancetta pan and cook for a further 2–3 minutes, or until the pancetta is crispy and brown.
4   Add the garlic to the onion and cook for 1–2 minutes, then add the paprika, double cream, thyme leaves, water and remaining corn. Stir well and cook over a medium heat for 10 minutes, or until the corn has softened and the sauce has thickened.
5   Meanwhile, cook the green beans in boiling salted water until tender. Drain and put to one side until needed.
6   When the corn has softened, stir through the Parmesan, sour cream and chopped parsley and remove from the heat.
7   Pour the olive oil over the scallops, season with salt and pepper and gently mix until well coated. Place a large, non-stick frying pan over a medium–high heat. When hot, carefully add the scallops and cook for 1–2 minutes on one side, then flip over, add the butter to the pan and cook for a further minute. Baste the scallops with the butter and remove the pan from heat.
8   Spoon the creamed corn into shallow bowls and add the green beans. Top with the scallops and sprinkle with the pancetta and corn mixture before serving.

Squid and Fennel Stew

Serves 4

3 tbsp extra virgin olive oil, plus extra
    for drizzling
1 onion, peeled and diced
4 garlic cloves, peeled and finely
    sliced
1 small fennel bulb, trimmed
    and finely sliced
½ tsp chilli flakes
2 tsp fennel seeds
1 tsp sweet smoked paprika
3 rosemary sprigs, leaves finely
    chopped
150ml dry white wine
2 x 400g tins of chopped tomatoes
600g cleaned squid, or a mixture of
    cleaned squid and peeled prawns
2 x 400g tins of butter beans,
    drained and rinsed
100g pitted Kalamata olives
Small handful of flat leaf parsley,
    roughly chopped
Sea salt and freshly ground black
    pepper

This Mediterranean-style one-pot stew is crammed with flavour despite being so quick and easy to put together. Get your fishmonger to clean and prep the squid, or buy it ready prepared from a supermarket to reduce the amount of work you have to do to get dinner on the table. Serve it with fresh or toasted baguette to soak up the incredible sauce.

1   Place a large, non-stick sauté pan over a medium–high heat. When hot, add the oil and onion and sauté for 2–3 minutes. Add the garlic and sauté for 2 more minutes. Add the sliced fennel, chilli, fennel seeds, paprika and rosemary and cook for 3–4 minutes.

2   Increase the heat to high, add the wine and let it reduce by half before adding the tomatoes to the pan. Bring to a simmer and cook for 10 minutes.

3   Meanwhile, prepare your squid. Cut down the long side of each squid tube and open it out flat. Using a sharp knife, lightly score the inside of the flesh, then cut into 5–7cm pieces.

4   Add the squid to the pan and cook for 5–6 minutes, stirring occasionally.

5   Add the butter beans and olives and cook for a further 2–3 minutes. Season to taste, remove from the heat and stir in the parsley.

6   Spoon the stew into warm bowls, drizzle with extra virgin olive oil and serve with crusty bread and a simple salad.

Miso-glazed Cod

Serves 4

5 tbsp white miso paste

2 tbsp mirin

1½ tbsp sugar

1 tbsp soy sauce

3cm piece of fresh root ginger,
    peeled and finely grated

4 x 200g cod fillets, skin on and
    pin-boned

350g Tenderstem broccoli, trimmed

1 tbsp olive oil

For the cucumber pickle

1 cucumber

4 tbsp rice vinegar

1 tbsp caster sugar

Large pinch of salt

To serve

Pickled ginger

2 tbsp furikake seasoning

Japanese white miso has a wonderfully deep, savoury richness and makes a great glaze for fish like cod and salmon. In the not too distant past, it was available only in Asian shops or from specialist sites online, but these days it can be found in most supermarkets. You can use it to flavour soups or poaching broths, salad dressings, stir-fries or marinades, so keeping some in the fridge can be the starting point for many meals.

1   Preheat the oven to 240°C/220°C fan/Gas 9.

2   Combine the miso, mirin, sugar, soy sauce and ginger in a shallow dish just big enough to hold the four pieces of fish. Coat both sides of the fish in the marinade, then leave it to marinate, flesh side down, for 10 minutes.

3   Meanwhile, place the broccoli in a small baking tray in a single layer, drizzle over the olive oil and toss to coat.

4   To make the pickle, use a mandolin or food processor to slice the cucumber into very thin rounds. Place them in a bowl, add the rice vinegar, sugar and salt and mix well. Leave to sit for 10 minutes.

5   Put the fish onto a small baking tray and place on the top shelf of the oven along with the tray of broccoli and cook for 15 minutes.

6   Remove the fish from the oven. If there are any areas where the glaze hasn't browned, run a blowtorch over the surface until evenly coloured.

7   Drain the cucumber and plate the cod with the broccoli and a spoonful of pickled cucumber. Add some pickled ginger and sprinkle with furikake seasoning to serve.

Grilled Mackerel with Orange Gremolata Dressing

Serves 4

4 mackerel fillets, skin on
Olive oil, for grilling
Juice of 1 small orange
4 rosemary sprigs, chopped in half

For the orange gremolata dressing
100ml olive oil
2 garlic cloves, peeled and finely
  chopped
Zest and juice of 1 small orange
2 tbsp roughly chopped flat leaf
  parsley
Sea salt and freshly ground black
  pepper

Time-saving tip
Slash the skin of the mackerel several times, as this allows the heat to penetrate to the centre of the fish and speeds up the cooking.

We spend a lot of time as a family in Cornwall, where the fish is amazing. In fact, we barbecue fresh mackerel throughout the summer, and this orange gremolata is one of our favourite accompaniments. It's quick to put together and packs a citrus punch that goes really well with the oily fish.

1 Preheat the grill to medium–high. Line the grill pan with foil.
2 To make the orange gremolata dressing, put all the ingredients for it into a bowl and season with salt and pepper. Mix well, then put to one side.
3 Using a sharp knife, score the skin on the mackerel fillets, then place them on the prepared grill pan, skin side down. Drizzle olive oil over each of the fillets, add a squeeze of orange juice and scatter the rosemary sprigs on top.
4 Place the pan under the grill and cook the fish for 1–2 minutes before turning over and cooking for another 4–5 minutes, or until the skin is crisp and the flesh is opaque.
5 Transfer the fish to a platter and spoon over the gremolata dressing, before serving with a large green salad and lots of warm crusty bread.

Malaysian Fish and Okra Curry

Serves 4

2 tbsp vegetable oil

1 onion, peeled and finely diced

3 garlic cloves, peeled and finely chopped

3cm piece of fresh root ginger, peeled and finely grated

1 long red chilli, deseeded if you want a milder hit, finely chopped

1 tsp Thai shrimp paste

1 heaped tsp ground turmeric

2 tomatoes, roughly chopped

250ml fish stock

400ml coconut cream

1 kaffir lime leaf

2 tsp lemongrass paste

1 tsp coconut palm sugar

1 tbsp tamarind paste

650g monkfish fillets

200g okra

2 tbsp chopped coriander

When you are tempted to order a takeaway, remember that this knockout Malaysian fish curry can be ready in just 30 minutes. It will be on the table before the delivery driver even sets off to your house! And this light but creamy, sweet-and-sour curry will blow most takeaways out of the water. I know that okra is a bit of a divisive vegetable, so leave it out if you don't like it.

1 Place a large, non-stick sauté pan over a medium–high heat and add the oil. When hot, add the onion and cook for 2–3 minutes, or until softened.

2 Add the garlic, ginger and chilli, and cook for 2 minutes before adding the shrimp paste and turmeric. Stir for 1 minute, or until fragrant, then add the tomatoes, fish stock, coconut cream, kaffir lime leaf, lemongrass paste, palm sugar and tamarind paste. Stir well, bring to the boil and simmer for 10–12 minutes.

3 Meanwhile, cut the monkfish into 3–5cm pieces. Trim the okra and cut each one in half at an angle.

4 Add the okra to the pan and cook for 2 minutes, then add the monkfish and cook for a further 5–6 minutes, or until cooked through. Remove the pan from the heat, stir in the coriander and serve in bowls with basmati rice or Aromatic Saffron Pilaf (see page 210).

Tuna Steaks with Preserved Lemon Couscous

Serves 2

2 x 200g tuna steaks
1 tbsp olive oil

For the preserved lemon couscous
100g couscous
Pinch of saffron
½ preserved lemon, finely chopped
150ml vegetable stock
¼ cucumber
2 tbsp coriander leaves
2 tbsp mint leaves
1 x 400g tin of chickpeas, drained
   and rinsed
2 tbsp extra virgin olive oil
Lemon juice, to taste
Sea salt and freshly ground black
   pepper

To serve
½ tsp sumac
Lemon wedges

> **If you have more time...**
> ... make the Moroccan Carrot
> Salad on page 205 to go with
> this. It will turn a simple lunch
> into a feast.

All types of fish are quick to cook, but tuna wins the speed prize because it's served rare in the middle and is literally in and out of the pan in four minutes. These steaks are seasoned with sumac, which has a lemony tang. It offsets the meaty tuna brilliantly and complements the Moroccan flavours in the couscous.

1   Put the couscous into a heatproof bowl. Using a pestle and mortar, grind the saffron to a powder, then place in a small saucepan with the preserved lemon and vegetable stock. Bring to the boil and pour over the couscous. Stir well, cover the bowl with cling film and leave to sit for 5–10 minutes.

2   Meanwhile, finely dice the cucumber and roughly chop the herbs.

3   Uncover the couscous and fluff it up with a fork. Add the cucumber, herbs, chickpeas, extra virgin olive oil and a little lemon juice. Mix well and season with salt and pepper. Set aside.

4   Place a large, non-stick frying pan over a medium–high heat. Drizzle the tuna steaks with the olive oil and season both sides with salt and pepper. When the pan is smoking hot, add the tuna and cook for 2 minutes on each side.

5   Spoon the couscous onto plates and place the tuna on top. Sprinkle each plate with the sumac and serve with lemon wedges and a green salad.

Baked Sea Bream with Fennel, Carrot and Lemon

Serves 2

1 large carrot
2 baby fennel bulbs
2 tbsp olive oil
Zest and juice of 1 lemon
2 x 120g sea bream fillets
1 tsp fennel pollen (optional)
Sea salt and freshly ground
   black pepper

Time-saving tip

Using a mandolin or vegetable peeler to cut vegetables into ribbons means they will cook more quickly than if you slice them. You can also serve them raw for a crunchy salad.

I have seasoned these sea bream fillets with fennel pollen, which is exactly what it sounds like – the pollen from fennel flowers, which has been sun-dried in southern Italy. I have made it optional as it's an expensive ingredient, but you need only a little because it's so intense and a little goes a long way. Its aniseed flavour goes wonderfully with fish, chicken and pork, and is also good lightly sprinkled over salads or couscous.

1 Preheat the oven to 200°C/180°C fan/Gas 6.
2 Cut two pieces of baking paper about 35 x 40cm, and fold each one in half lengthways.
3 Peel the carrot and use a mandolin or vegetable peeler to slice into fine ribbons. Trim the fennel, reserving any fronds, and finely slice the bulb into ribbons.
4 Divide the vegetables between the two pieces of baking paper, placing them to the right of the fold. Pour over a tablespoon of oil, then sprinkle with any reserved fronds and the lemon zest.
5 Using a sharp knife, score the sea bream skin, then place a fish fillet on top of the vegetables, skin side up, and season with salt and pepper. Squeeze the lemon juice over each fillet, then sprinkle with the fennel pollen (if using).
6 Fold the baking paper over the fish and seal the long edges together by folding them over each other. Twist the ends and tuck them underneath. Put the parcels on a baking tray and place on the top shelf of the oven for 8–10 minutes, or until the fish is cooked through.
7 Serve the sea bream in the paper bags with new potatoes and a green salad.

Garlic and Chilli Prawns

Serves 2

4 tbsp olive oil

6 garlic cloves, peeled and finely
chopped

1 red chilli, deseeded if you want
a milder hit, finely chopped

Pinch of chilli flakes (optional)

600g raw tiger prawns

80ml manzanilla sherry

1 tsp tomato purée

200g cherry tomatoes, quartered

25g butter, cut into 1cm cubes

2 tbsp chopped flat leaf parsley

Sea salt and freshly ground black
pepper

Prawns – in fact, shellfish in general – are the perfect fast food because they take just a few minutes to cook. All the work here is in chopping the garlic and chilli and quartering the tomatoes. Make sure you serve these lip-smackingly good prawns with plenty of good bread for mopping up all the juices, and a lot of paper napkins as things could get messy...

1 Place a large, non-stick frying pan over a medium–high heat and add the oil. When hot, add the garlic, chilli and chilli flakes (if using), and stir gently for 1 minute.

2 Add the prawns and cook until pink on one side. Turn each of the prawns over and add the sherry, tomato purée and cherry tomatoes. Cook for 1–2 minutes, or until the prawns are pink all over, then transfer the prawns to a plate. Continue to cook the mixture in the pan for 2–3 more minutes, until the tomatoes have softened.

3 Return the prawns to the pan, stir in the butter and parsley, and season to taste. Serve with a green salad and some crusty bread to mop up the delicious sauce.

Pan-fried Salmon with Warm Potato Salad

Serves 4

700g new or salad potatoes, such
   as Charlotte or Pink Fir Apple
½ tsp salt
1 bay leaf
2 thyme sprigs
5 black peppercorns
1 tbsp olive oil
4 salmon fillets, skin on
2 banana shallots
2 tbsp dill
150g crème fraîche
2 tbsp nonpareille capers
Sea salt and freshly ground black
   pepper
Lemon wedges, to serve

This dish might seem a little old-fashioned, but I don't think you can beat a simple, unadorned piece of salmon with warm potatoes dressed Scandinavian style with crème fraîche, capers and dill. Make sure you choose the freshest, most ethically sourced salmon possible, and don't overcook it – the skin should be crisp but the flesh should still be a little translucent in the middle.

1   Bring a kettle of water to the boil, then pour it into a saucepan. Add the potatoes, salt, bay leaf, thyme sprigs and peppercorns, cover the pan with a lid and bring to the boil. Once boiling, remove the lid, reduce the heat and simmer for 10–12 minutes, or until cooked through.

2   While the potatoes are cooking, peel and finely chop the shallots and chop the dill.

3   Once the potatoes are cooked, drain and lay them out on a chopping board to cool a little. Discard the bay leaf, thyme twigs and peppercorns.

4   Place a large frying pan over a medium–high heat and add the olive oil. Season the salmon fillets with salt and, once the oil is hot, add them to the pan, skin side down. Cook for 3–4 minutes before turning over and cooking for another 1–2 minutes. Remove the pan from the heat and set to one side.

5   Using a clean tea towel to protect your hand, slice the hot potatoes and put them into a bowl with the shallots, dill, crème fraîche and capers. Stir to combine, and season generously with salt and black pepper.

6   Place the salmon fillets on plates with a lemon wedge alongside, and add a generous spoonful of the warm potatoes. Serve with a green salad.

Chinese-style Baked Sea Bass

Serves 2

4 baby pak choi, cut in half
   lengthways
125g fine green beans, trimmed
100g baby corn, larger ones halved
   lengthways
2 x 180g sea bass fillets, skin on
5cm piece of fresh root ginger,
   peeled and julienned
2 garlic cloves, peeled and finely
   sliced
1 long red chilli, deseeded if you
   want a milder hit, finely sliced
½ tsp cornflour
2 tbsp soy sauce
1 tbsp oyster sauce
1 tbsp sesame oil, plus extra to serve
4 tbsp Shaoxing rice wine
Pinch of ground white pepper
Jasmine rice, to serve

Cooking fish in a bag (en papillote) is a great way to impart flavour into the flesh, and there is the added bonus of very little mess to wash up afterwards. Here I have seasoned the sea bass with ginger, chilli and garlic as well as rice wine, sesame oil and oyster sauce, so the aroma that hits you when you open the bag is sensational.

1 Preheat the oven to 220°C/200°C fan/Gas 7.
2 Cut two pieces of baking paper about 35 x 40cm, and fold each one in half lengthways. Lay the pak choi to the right of each fold. Put the beans on top, then place the corn on top of the beans.
3 Cut each sea bass fillet in half across the middle and place two halves, overlapping slightly, on top of the vegetables.
4 Sprinkle the ginger, garlic and chilli over the fish.
5 Put the cornflour in a bowl with the soy sauce and mix until well combined. Add the oyster sauce, sesame oil, rice wine and white pepper and mix again. Spoon the mixture over the fish.
6 Fold the baking paper over the fish and seal the edges together by folding them over each other. Twist the ends and tuck them underneath. Put the parcels on a baking tray and place on the top shelf of the oven for 15 minutes.
7 Place the parcels on two serving plates, open them up and drizzle with a little extra sesame oil before serving with jasmine rice.

Salt and Pink Pepper Prawns with Lime Mayonnaise

Serves 4

1 tbsp pink peppercorns
½ tsp sea salt
Zest and juice of 2 limes
3 tbsp olive oil
500g raw, peeled king prawns
1 tbsp roughly chopped coriander

For the lime mayonnaise
100g mayonnaise
Juice of 1 lime

Pink peppercorns aren't technically peppercorns at all; they're actually a type of berry, but they have a peppery taste and aroma, and, although a bit milder, can be used in many of the same dishes as regular pepper. Here the combination of pink pepper, lime and coriander marries beautifully with the sweetness of the prawns for a cracking starter or main course.

1 Using a pestle and mortar, grind the peppercorns and salt into a coarse powder.
2 Put the lime zest and juice into a large bowl, then stir in the olive oil and pink pepper mixture.
3 Add the prawns and, using clean hands, toss gently until they are well coated.
4 Mix the mayonnaise and lime juice together in a small bowl.
5 Place a large, non-stick frying pan over a medium–high heat and, when very hot, add the prawns. Cook for 2–3 minutes, stirring regularly, until all the prawns are pink and cooked through.
6 Tip the prawns onto a platter, sprinkle with the coriander and serve immediately with the lime mayonnaise and a big green salad.

Roast Hake with Saffron Mayonnaise

Serves 4

300g Tenderstem broccoli
4 x 200g hake fillets, skinned and
  pin-boned
1 tbsp thyme leaves
2 tbsp extra virgin olive oil
Zest and juice of ½ orange
1 lemon, cut into wedges

For the saffron mayonnaise
Pinch of saffron
1 tbsp boiling water
2 egg yolks
2 small garlic cloves, peeled and
  crushed
1 tbsp Dijon mustard
80ml olive oil
80ml vegetable oil
Lemon juice, to taste
Sea salt and freshly ground black
  pepper

Chef's tip
Grinding your saffron threads
in a mortar and pouring over a
little hot water before using will
get the maximum flavour out
of this expensive spice.

Hake is a meaty white fish with a mild flavour that is increasingly replacing less-sustainable haddock and cod on menus. I love it for its slightly sweet-tasting flesh and its ability to take on other flavours as diverse as chorizo, black pudding and, as here, orange and saffron. I know it's easier to open a jar of mayo than to make your own, but the flavour of home-made is incomparable, so give this a go.

1 Preheat the oven to 200°C/180°C fan/Gas 6.
2 Using a pestle and mortar, grind the saffron to a powder, then add the boiling water and leave to sit.
3 Put the broccoli into a large roasting tray and place the hake fillets on top, skin side down. Sprinkle with the thyme, salt and pepper, then drizzle with the olive oil. Add a little orange zest to each piece of hake.
4 Place the tray in the oven on a high shelf for 10–15 minutes, or until the fish is cooked through and the broccoli is slightly charred.
5 Meanwhile, make the mayonnaise. Put the egg yolks, garlic and mustard into a bowl. Whisk well, then pour the two oils into the bowl in a gentle stream while whisking constantly. Add the saffron water and a little salt and pepper and whisk again. Add lemon juice to taste.
6 Remove the hake from oven and squeeze over the orange juice. Leave to rest for 2–3 minutes, then serve with a big dollop of the saffron mayonnaise and a lemon wedge on each plate.

Poultry

Saffron Chicken Flatbreads with Minted Yoghurt 79

Asian Duck Salad 80

Moroccan Chicken Traybake 83

Buffalo Chicken and Blue Cheese Dressing 84

Wild Garlic Turkey Kievs 87

Chinese-style Ginger Chicken with Garlic Rice 88

Crispy Chicken Thighs with Romesco Sauce 91

Double Lemon Chicken 92

Thai Chilli and Basil Chicken 95

Chicken Ramen 96

Pan-seared Duck Breast with Pak Choi and Orange Sauce 99

Pancetta-wrapped Guinea Fowl with Glazed Carrots and Mustard Sauce 100

Saffron Chicken Flatbreads with Minted Yoghurt

Serves 2

Pinch of saffron

1 tbsp boiling water

500g boneless, skinless chicken thighs

2 garlic cloves, peeled and crushed

1 tsp thyme leaves

Zest of 1 lemon

4 tbsp Greek yoghurt

1 red onion, peeled and cut into 8 wedges

2 flatbreads

2 large handfuls of mixed salad leaves

140g cherry tomatoes, halved

2 tbsp crispy fried onions (available from supermarkets), to serve (optional)

For the minted yoghurt

150g Greek yoghurt

Small handful of mint leaves, finely chopped

Lemon juice, to taste

Chef's tip

Whenever using wooden skewers for grilling or barbecuing, you will need to soak them in water for at least 30 minutes in advance of cooking or they will burn.

When we're in LA, we like to barbecue almost all year round, and chicken on sticks is a family favourite, probably because it's so easy and there are endless variations. I love using the mild-mannered spice saffron, which stains the meat golden yellow and imparts a gentle Mediterranean scent to everything. The fresh minted yoghurt is the perfect accompaniment, but you could replace it with tzatziki if you're in a rush.

1 Soak 4 bamboo skewers in water for at least 30 minutes. Preheat the oven to 240°C/220°C fan/Gas 9.

2 Using a pestle and mortar, grind the saffron to a powder, then cover with the boiling water and leave to sit.

3 Cut the chicken into 5cm pieces and place in a bowl with the garlic, thyme, lemon zest and yoghurt. Season with salt and pepper, add the saffron water and mix well.

4 Thread the chicken pieces onto the skewers, alternating them with the red onion. Place on a non-stick roasting tray and put on a high shelf in the oven for 12 minutes.

5 Meanwhile, make the minted yoghurt. Combine the yoghurt with the mint, add lemon juice to taste and season with a little salt and pepper. Set aside until needed.

6 Put the flatbreads on a baking tray and place in the bottom of the oven to warm for a few minutes.

7 Preheat the grill. When the chicken has been cooking for 12 minutes, place it under the grill and cook for a further 3–4 minutes, until golden brown and cooked through.

8 Put the flatbreads on plates and spread some of the minted yoghurt down the middle. Add a handful of the salad leaves to each and divide the tomatoes between them. Put the cooked skewers on top and sprinkle with fried onions to serve.

Asian Duck Salad

Serves 2

2 duck breasts

1 tsp Chinese five-spice powder

6 radishes, finely sliced

⅓ cucumber, halved lengthways and sliced at an angle

2 large handfuls of watercress

2 large handfuls of beansprouts

2 large handfuls of mixed salad leaves

Small handful of coriander leaves

1 tsp toasted sesame seeds

1 long red chilli, deseeded if you want a milder hit, finely sliced at an angle

2 spring onions, green parts only, finely sliced lengthways

Sea salt and freshly ground black pepper

For the dressing

1½ tbsp hoisin sauce

1 tsp peeled and grated fresh root ginger

1 tbsp sesame oil

1 tbsp rice vinegar

Juice of ½ lime

Time-saving tip

When you are grating ingredients, such as ginger, lime zest or cheese, grate onto a plate rather than a chopping board. It's much quicker and easier to tip the ingredient into the pan, and you don't leave half of it behind on the board.

Duck is quite a dense meat, but because it's served pink in the middle, it's relatively quick to cook.
The robust, gamey flavour of the duck goes brilliantly with Chinese five-spice, which is a mix of star anise, Chinese cinnamon, Sichuan pepper, cloves and fennel seed. It gives an instant Asian vibe to stir-fries, ribs, chicken wings and pork, or use it in baking to add a new dimension to cakes and fruit puddings.

1 Preheat the oven to 200°C/180°C fan/Gas 6.

2 Using a very sharp knife, score the skin on the duck breasts in diagonal lines, first in one direction, then the other so you have a diamond pattern. Rub in the Chinese five-spice, then season both sides with salt and pepper.

3 Put the duck breasts, skin side down, in a non-stick, ovenproof frying pan. Place the pan over a medium–high heat and cook for 7 minutes, or until the fat has rendered and the skin is crisp and golden.

4 Meanwhile, put the radishes and cucumber into a salad bowl with the watercress, beansprouts, mixed salad leaves and coriander.

5 Make the dressing by whisking all the ingredients together.

6 Turn the duck breasts over and place the frying pan in the oven for 3–4 minutes. Remove from the oven and leave to rest for 2–3 minutes.

7 Add half the dressing to the salad bowl and mix well. Divide the salad between two serving plates.

8 Carve the duck into thick slices and arrange on top of the salad. Spoon over the remaining dressing and sprinkle with the sesame seeds, chilli and spring onions before serving.

Moroccan Chicken Traybake

Serves 4

200g baby carrots
2 red onions, peeled and each
    cut into 8 wedges
2 tbsp olive oil
2 tbsp ras-el-hanout
200ml chicken stock
150g couscous
4 chicken breasts, skin on
2 courgettes
1 x 400g tin of chickpeas,
    drained and rinsed
50ml water
4 tbsp chopped coriander
Lemon juice, to taste
15g nibbed pistachios, roughly
    chopped
Sea salt and freshly ground black
    pepper
Rose petals, to serve (optional)

Using a spice mix like ras-el-hanout is a great kitchen shortcut – just sprinkle it over the vegetables and chicken in this easy traybake and you will be instantly transported to the souks of Morocco or Tunis without any effort at all. However, keep an eye on the sell-by date of ground spices – after a year or two they lose their potency, so don't let them languish in the back of your cupboard for more than a decade and then expect them to taste of anything.

1 Preheat the oven to 220°C/200°C fan/Gas 7.
2 Wash the baby carrots, cutting any larger ones in half lengthways. Place in a large roasting tray with the onions. Drizzle with 1 tablespoon of the olive oil and sprinkle over 1 tablespoon of ras-el-hanout until evenly coated. Place in the oven for 10 minutes.
3 Pour the chicken stock into a small pan, place over a medium–high heat and bring to the boil. Put the couscous into a bowl with a little salt and pepper. Pour the hot stock over it, cover with cling film and set aside to absorb the liquid.
4 Score the chicken skin with a sharp knife, then season with salt and pepper and sprinkle over ½ tablespoon ras-el-hanout.
5 Cut each courgette into quarters lengthways and then into 5cm lengths, then sprinkle with the remaining ½ tablespoon ras-el-hanout. Remove the tray from the oven and add the courgettes and chickpeas. Place the chicken breasts on top and drizzle with the remaining tablespoon of olive oil. Add the water to the bottom of the pan and return to the oven on a high shelf for 15 minutes.
6 Meanwhile, uncover the couscous and fluff it up with a fork. Stir in the coriander, then add lemon juice and salt and pepper to taste.
7 Remove the roasting tray from the oven and sprinkle with pistachios and rose petals (if using). Bring to the table and serve straight from the tray.

Buffalo Chicken and Blue Cheese Dressing

Serves 2

8 chicken mini fillets
300ml buttermilk
1½ tsp garlic granules
1½ tsp onion powder
1 tsp dried thyme
½ tsp cayenne pepper
Vegetable oil, for frying
150g plain flour
80ml RedHot Wings Sauce
Sea salt and freshly ground
   black pepper

For the dressing
50g Greek yoghurt
50g sour cream
1 tbsp mayonnaise
35g blue cheese, crumbled
Squeeze of lemon juice
2 dashes of Worcestershire sauce

To serve
Celery sticks
Little gem lettuce leaves

If you have more time…
… leave the chicken fillets in the
buttermilk marinade overnight;
they will be even more tender
when it comes to cooking them.

As I spend a lot of time in the United States these days and have eight restaurants there now, I have become partial to some of the classic foods of America. This is my take on buffalo chicken with blue cheese dip and hot sauce, and it is finger-licking good, if I say so myself. Using mini fillets keeps the cooking time short, and they are easy to pick up and eat without getting yourself into a sticky mess.

1   Preheat the oven to 140°C/120°C fan/Gas 1.
2   Put the chicken into a bowl with the buttermilk, garlic granules, onion powder, thyme, cayenne pepper and a little salt and pepper. Mix well.
3   Heat a one-third depth of oil in a large pan to 190°C, or until a cube of bread browns in 25 seconds.
4   Meanwhile, mix all the dressing ingredients together. Season to taste.
5   Put the flour into a shallow bowl, add some salt and pepper and mix well. Take a mini fillet out of the marinade, keeping as much buttermilk on it as possible, and coat in the flour. Transfer to a plate while you repeat this step with 3 more fillets.
6   Once the oil has reached temperature, carefully add the coated fillets and cook for 4–5 minutes, or until deep golden brown and cooked through. Drain on kitchen paper, then transfer to a baking tray and place in the oven to keep warm.
7   Flour the remaining chicken fillets while you bring the oil back up to temperature. When it's hot enough, carefully add the fillets and cook for 4–5 minutes. Drain on kitchen paper, then keep warm with the other fillets.
8   Pour the Red Hot Wings Sauce and blue cheese dressing into serving bowls, and serve alongside the chicken with celery sticks and lettuce.

Wild Garlic Turkey Kievs

Serves 2

100g butter, softened
2 tbsp roughly chopped tarragon
Zest of ½ lemon
2 small garlic cloves, peeled and
    crushed
Large handful of wild garlic, roughly
    chopped
1 egg
50g plain flour
50ml milk
75g panko breadcrumbs
1 tbsp finely chopped flat leaf parsley
    or dill
4 x 100g turkey escalopes
150g fine green beans, trimmed
Vegetable oil, for frying
Sea salt and freshly ground black
    pepper

It's back to the 1970s with this retro dish, but these days I use turkey (the breasts are so much bigger and easier to work with) and wild garlic for a more subtle, sophisticated flavour. If it isn't wild garlic season and you haven't got any wild garlic butter in the freezer (see Tip, page 47), add another regular garlic clove to the recipe.

1   Put the butter, tarragon, lemon zest, garlic and wild garlic into a small food processor. Season with a little salt and pepper and blend until well combined.

2   Put the egg, flour and milk in a shallow bowl and whisk together to make a batter.

3   Mix the panko breadcrumbs with the parsley in a second shallow bowl.

4   Lay 2 of the escalopes on a piece of cling film so that they are slightly overlapping. Bash them lightly with a rolling pin to join them together and to make the meat an even thickness.

5   Put half the wild garlic butter on one half of the joined escalope, leaving a 1.5cm border around it. Spread a little batter all the way around the edges, then fold the escalope over the garlic butter and press down to seal well. Repeat steps 4 and 5 with the remaining escalopes.

6   Dip each Kiev in the batter, making sure they are coated evenly, then cover in the panko breadcrumbs. Place them into the fridge for 5 minutes.

7   Meanwhile, cook the green beans in salted boiling water until tender. Drain and keep warm until needed.

8   Place a sauté pan over a medium–high heat and add a 2cm depth of oil. When hot, carefully place each Kiev in the oil and cook for 3–4 minutes on each side, or until deep golden and cooked through. Drain on kitchen paper and serve immediately with the green beans.

Chinese-style Ginger Chicken with Garlic Rice

Serves 4

4 chicken breasts, skin on
4cm piece of fresh root ginger,
   peeled and julienned
6 spring onions – 4 trimmed
   and cut in half; 2, green part
   only, finely sliced, to serve
500ml chicken stock
2 tbsp Shaoxing rice wine
1 tbsp light soy sauce
Sea salt

For the garlic rice
260g jasmine rice
1 tbsp vegetable oil
1 tbsp sesame oil
3 large garlic cloves, peeled
   and finely chopped
500ml chicken stock
Pinch of ground white pepper

For many people, chicken is the mainstay of the midweek supper, and I think some of us are always on the lookout for new and interesting ways of serving it. This recipe is quick, full of flavour and bound to be popular. Crisping the skin as described is a really easy trick for adding crunch and flavour. It's not an essential step but it will take this dish to the next level.

1 Preheat the oven to 200°C/180°C fan/Gas 6.
2 Remove the skin from the chicken breasts and scrape any excess fat off it with a sharp knife. Season both sides of the skin with salt and place on a baking tray. Place another baking tray on top to keep the skin flat and place in the oven for 12–15 minutes, or until golden and crisp. Set aside to cool.
3 Put the chicken breasts, ginger, spring onion halves and 500ml chicken stock into a saucepan, place over a high heat and bring to the boil.
4 Meanwhile, wash the jasmine rice three times and drain thoroughly. Heat the vegetable oil and sesame oil in a saucepan, then add the garlic and cook for 2 minutes. Add the rice, 500ml chicken stock and the pepper and bring to the boil. Place a lid on the pan, reduce the heat to low and simmer for 5–8 minutes, or until the rice is cooked.
5 Once the chicken pan is boiling, reduce the heat and simmer gently for 5 minutes. Remove the chicken from the pan and set aside to rest. Discard the spring onions, then rapidly return the stock to the boil. Add the Shaoxing wine and soy sauce and cook for another 5 minutes.
6 Spoon the rice into bowls, then slice the chicken and lay it on top. Ladle the stock over and garnish with the spring onion greens. Crumble a piece of chicken skin over each bowl to serve.

Crispy Chicken Thighs with Romesco Sauce

Serves 2

4 chicken thighs, bone in and skin on
2 tbsp olive oil
100g cavolo nero
1 tbsp water
120g padrón peppers
Sea salt and freshly ground black
   pepper

For the sauce
150g roasted peppers, from a jar
1 garlic clove, peeled and crushed
20g toasted blanched almonds
1 tbsp sherry vinegar
¼ tsp sweet smoked paprika
20g sourdough bread, crust removed
40ml extra virgin olive oil

Romesco is a vibrant red pepper sauce given texture by blitzed almonds. It's a dream with chicken, but it can also be served with fish, prawns and roasted leeks or calçots – the large spring onions from Catalonia in Spain, where the sauce comes from. Brilliantly, you can buy roasted red peppers in a jar, so you don't have to prepare them yourself, making this sauce almost completely hassle-free.

1   Preheat the oven to 200°C/180°C fan/Gas 6.

2   Season the chicken thighs with salt and pepper. Place a large, ovenproof frying pan over a high heat. When hot, add 1 tablespoon of the olive oil and put the chicken thighs in skin side down. Reduce the heat to medium and cook the chicken for 8 minutes.

3   Once the chicken skin is golden brown and crisp, turn the thighs over and add the cavolo nero and water. Season with a little salt and pepper, then place the whole pan in the oven for 8 minutes.

4   Meanwhile, place all the romesco sauce ingredients in a small food processor with a little salt and pepper, and blend until smooth.

5   Place a small frying pan over a high heat. When very hot, add the remaining tablespoon of olive oil, the padrón peppers and a sprinkle of salt. Cook for 4–5 minutes, or until the skin on the peppers has blistered and softened.

6   Remove the chicken from the pan and set aside to rest. Mix the cavolo nero into the pan juices and serve with the chicken, padrón peppers and a generous spoonful of the romesco sauce.

Double Lemon Chicken

Serves 4

2 tbsp olive oil

8 chicken thighs, bone in and skin on

5 garlic cloves, peeled and crushed
with the blade of a chef's knife

3 thyme sprigs

1 fresh lemon

1 preserved lemon

1 tbsp sherry vinegar

2 tbsp dark soy sauce

3½ tbsp runny honey

1 tbsp water

2 tbsp roughly chopped flat leaf
parsley

Sea salt and freshly ground black
pepper

Chef's tip

To get more juice out of a lemon,
heat it in the microwave for
20 seconds on full power before
squeezing it. The heat helps
break down the membranes in
the fruit, which means the juice
is released more easily.

Lemon and chicken is a classic pairing, but by adding
both fresh and preserved lemons to this recipe, the
lemon flavour is intensified and it becomes something
new. The almost molten sauce is sweet, sticky and
utterly delicious. Serve with mashed potatoes (see
page 213), lightly cooked green vegetables or a simple
salad to counterbalance the richness.

1   Preheat the oven to 200°C/180°C fan/Gas 6.

2   Place a large ovenproof frying pan over a high heat
    and, when hot, add the olive oil. Season the chicken
    thighs with salt and pepper and add them to the pan
    with the garlic and thyme sprigs. Cook for 2–3 minutes
    on each side, or until golden brown.

3   Meanwhile, slice the fresh lemon very finely on
    a mandolin, and roughly chop the preserved lemon.

4   Add the sherry vinegar to the frying pan and allow
    to reduce by half before adding the soy sauce and
    honey. Shake the pan to mix the sauce and reduce
    the heat to medium–high.

5   Pour in the tablespoon of water, then add the fresh
    and preserved lemons and bring to a simmer and
    place in the oven for 10–15 minutes, or until the
    chicken is cooked through and the sauce has reduced
    to a thick syrup.

6   Transfer the chicken to a serving dish and sprinkle
    with the parsley before serving with green vegetables
    or a salad.

Thai Chilli and Basil Chicken

Serves 4

350g jasmine rice
600ml water
3 skinless, boneless chicken breasts, finely sliced
5 garlic cloves, peeled and finely chopped
4 Thai bird's-eye chillies, finely sliced
1 onion, peeled and thickly sliced
150g Tenderstem broccoli, cut into 5cm lengths
150g fine green beans, trimmed and halved
About 4 tbsp vegetable oil
2 tbsp oyster sauce
1 tbsp soy sauce
80ml chicken stock
2 tbsp fish sauce
1 tbsp caster sugar
1 tbsp cornflour
1 tbsp water
Large handful of Thai basil leaves
Small handful of regular basil leaves
Sea salt and ground white pepper

Thai basil is woodier and more robust than regular Italian basil, and has a spicy aniseed flavour that is quite distinct from its European cousin's. It isn't always easy to get hold of, but it's worth trying to track down to experience for yourself. When stir-frying, efficiency is everything – get all your ingredients prepped before you start and the process of getting dinner on the table will be seamless.

1 Wash the rice three times until the water runs clear, then place in a saucepan with the measured water and a pinch of salt. Bring to the boil, then reduce the heat to a low simmer and place a lid on the pan. Cook for a further 10–12 minutes, or until the liquid has gone and the rice is cooked.

2 Meanwhile, prepare the meat and all the vegetables for the stir-fry. Season the chicken with salt and white pepper.

3 Place a wok over a very high heat until smoking hot. Add 1 tablespoon vegetable oil and stir-fry a quarter of the chicken for 1 minute, or until it has browned lightly. Quickly remove the wok from the heat and transfer the chicken to a plate. Return the wok to the heat and cook the remaining chicken in the same way, adding more oil as necessary.

4 Combine the oyster sauce, soy sauce, chicken stock, fish sauce and sugar in a small bowl. In a separate bowl, mix the cornflour with the water.

5 Put the wok back on the heat, adding more oil as necessary, then stir-fry the garlic and half the chillies for 1 minute.

6 Add the onion and stir-fry for 2 minutes. Add the broccoli and green beans and cook for 2 minutes, adding a little water if they begin to stick.

7 Return the chicken to the wok and cook for a further 2–3 minutes.

8 Stir in the cornflour paste and Thai basil leaves and cook for 1 more minute.

9 Spoon the rice and stir-fry into bowls and sprinkle with the remaining chillies and basil leaves before serving.

Chicken Ramen

Serves 2

2 eggs

2 tbsp vegetable oil

2 chicken breasts, skin on

100g ramen noodles

2 large handfuls of baby spinach

2 large handfuls of beansprouts

1 litre chicken stock

1 tbsp white miso paste

2 tsp dashi powder

2 tbsp soy sauce

3 garlic cloves, peeled and finely
sliced

4cm piece of fresh root ginger,
peeled and julienned

2 tbsp saké (Japanese rice wine)

1 long red chilli, deseeded if you
want a milder hit, finely sliced
at an angle

2 spring onions, trimmed and finely
sliced at an angle

1 tsp furikake seasoning

Sea salt and ground white pepper

Sesame oil, to serve

Originally an import from China, the Japanese have made this noodle soup their own by flavouring the broth with ingredients such as miso, kombu and katsuobushi (dried tuna flakes). I use miso and dashi powder to give it that authentic taste, both of which are available from Asian supermarkets or online. In Japan, it isn't rude to slurp as you eat the noodles or to put the bowl to your lips to drink the last bit of the soup, so feel free!

1   Bring a kettle of water to the boil, pour into a saucepan and bring back to the boil over a high heat. Gently lower the eggs into it and cook for 5–6 minutes for a slightly runny yolk.

2   Meanwhile, put the vegetable oil in a non-stick frying pan and place over a high heat. Season the chicken breasts with salt and a little white pepper and place in the pan, skin side down. Cook over a medium heat for 4–5 minutes on one side.

3   Using a slotted spoon, transfer the eggs to a bowl of cold water to stop them cooking.

4   Add some salt to the water in the saucepan and bring back to the boil. Add the noodles and cook for 3–4 minutes, or until just tender. Drain and divide between two serving bowls. Add a handful of baby spinach and a handful of beansprouts to each bowl.

5   Carefully peel the eggs and cut them in half lengthways.

6   Pour the chicken stock into a saucepan, add the miso paste, dashi powder and soy sauce, then place the pan over a medium heat.

7   Turn the chicken breasts over and add the garlic and ginger to the pan. Cook for another 2–3 minutes, stirring the garlic and ginger often. Add the saké and cook for another 2 minutes.

8   When the chicken is cooked, remove it from the pan to rest. Add the pan juices, along with the garlic and ginger, to the chicken stock and stir well.

9   Slice the chicken and place on top of the noodles. Ladle over the stock and garnish with the chilli, spring onions, microherbs and furikake seasoning. Add the halved eggs to the bowls, drizzle with a little sesame oil and serve.

Pan-seared Duck Breast with Pak Choi and Orange Sauce

Serves 4

4 duck breasts
4 pak choi, halved
250ml orange juice
50ml soy sauce
2cm piece of fresh root ginger,
   peeled and grated
50g butter
50g runny honey
1 tbsp black and white sesame seeds
Sea salt and freshly ground black
   pepper
Cooked rice, to serve

Chef's tip

Before measuring honey, coat
the measuring spoon or bowl with
a thin layer of flavourless cooking
oil, and the honey will slip straight
off into the pan or mixing bowl
without leaving a sticky mess
behind. It's more accurate too.

Duck with orange is clearly a tried-and-tested combination, but adding soy sauce, honey and ginger gives it an Asian twist that freshens up the old French classic. Make sure you get quite a bit of colour on the pak choi before adding the sauce ingredients – the bitterness of the charred edges offsets the sweetness beautifully.

1 Preheat the oven to 200°C/180°C fan/Gas 6 and place a baking tray inside to heat up.
2 Using a very sharp knife, score the skin on the duck breasts in diagonal lines, first in one direction, then the other so you have a diamond pattern. Season well with salt and pepper.
3 Put the duck breasts, skin side down, in a non-stick, ovenproof frying pan. Place the pan over a medium–high heat and cook for 7 minutes, or until the fat has rendered and the skin is crisp and golden.
4 Turn the duck breasts over and place the frying pan in the oven for 3–4 minutes. Transfer the duck to a warm plate and leave to rest for 2–3 minutes.
5 Meanwhile, return the frying pan to the hob and add the halved pak choi. Cook for 2 minutes, or until beginning to colour, then add the orange juice, soy sauce, ginger and butter and bring to a simmer. Stir in the honey and reduce to a thick sauce.
6 To serve, slice the duck at an angle and plate up with the pak choi and some cooked rice. Pour over the sauce and sprinkle with the sesame seeds before serving.

Pancetta-wrapped Guinea Fowl with Glazed Carrots and Mustard Sauce

Serves 2

12 thin slices of pancetta

2 skinless guinea fowl breasts

1 tbsp mild olive oil

1 banana shallot, peeled and finely chopped

1 tsp wholegrain mustard

1 tsp Dijon mustard

1 tsp thyme leaves

50ml dry white wine

150ml chicken stock

125ml double cream

For the glazed carrots

300g Chantenay carrots

40g butter

250ml chicken stock

1 tsp honey

1 tbsp finely chopped flat leaf parsley

Sea salt and freshly ground black pepper

If you have more time...

... make the Garlic and Herb Mash (see page 213); it would go brilliantly with this richly flavoured dish.

I love guinea fowl – it's gamier and sweeter than chicken and feels more special. As the breasts are very lean, wrapping them in pancetta stops them drying out and adds a delicious salty crunch. Don't be tempted to cook the carrots in a saucepan – it is the wide surface area of the frying pan that allows the cooking liquor to reduce to a glaze.

1 Preheat the oven to 220°C/200°C fan/Gas 7.

2 Wash the carrots and put them into a large frying pan with the butter, chicken stock and honey. Add a little salt and pepper and place over a high heat. Bring to the boil, then reduce the heat to a strong simmer and cook for about 15 minutes, stirring occasionally, until the carrots are tender.

3 Meanwhile, lay 6 slices of pancetta on a chopping board, overlapping them slightly. Season the guinea fowl breasts and place one of them in the middle of the pancetta. Wrap the pancetta around it, then repeat this step with the second one.

4 Place a non-stick frying pan over a high heat. When hot, add the oil, then the guinea fowl breasts and cook for 2–3 minutes on each side, or until the pancetta is golden brown all over. Transfer to a small baking tray and place in the oven for 5 minutes.

5 Return the frying pan to the heat, add the shallot and cook for 2 minutes, or until softened. Stir in the mustards and thyme leaves, then add the wine and allow it to reduce by half over a high heat. Add the stock and cream, season with a little salt and pepper and reduce until the sauce thickens.

6 Remove the guinea fowl from the oven, keep warm and allow to rest for 10 minutes.

7 Check on the carrots – they should be cooked and the sauce should have reduced to a glaze. Stir in the parsley and remove the pan from the heat.

8 Serve the guinea fowl breasts with the glazed carrots, spooning the sauce over the top or serving it in small side dishes.

Meat

Steak Tacos with Pink Pickled Onion and Pico de Gallo 107

Pork Schnitzel with Celeriac Remoulade 108

Bacon Cheeseburgers with Pickled Cucumber Burger Sauce 111

Veal Scallopini with Mushroom Sauce 112

Sticky Pork with Asian Greens 115

Juniper Venison Steaks with Quick-braised Red Cabbage 116

Korean-style Lamb with Sesame Cucumber 119

Mexican Beef and Jalapeño Quesadillas 120

Minced Lamb Curry 123

Pork Larb with Sticky Coconut Rice 124

Veal Saltimbocca with Marsala Sauce 127

Mustard and Herb Meatballs with Balsamic Glaze and Parmesan Cheese 128

Rib-eye Steaks with Peppercorn Sauce 131

Roast Pork Chops with Crushed Charlotte Potatoes and Lettuce and Apple Salad 132

Lamb Rump with Creamed Cannellini Beans 135

Steak Tacos with Pink Pickled Onion and Pico de Gallo

Serves 2

2 x 220g bavette steaks
1 tsp ground cumin
1 tsp Mexican chilli powder
2 tbsp mild olive oil
6–8 x 15cm round Mexican corn
    or blue corn tortillas
Sea salt and freshly ground black
    pepper

For the pickled onion
2 red onions, peeled and finely sliced
¼ tsp dried oregano
Juice of 1 lime

For the pico de gallo
200g cherry tomatoes, quartered
1 green jalapeño chilli, deseeded
    if you want a milder hit, sliced
Small handful of coriander, roughly
    chopped
1 ripe avocado, peeled, stoned
    and diced
Squeeze of lime juice

For the chipotle crema
150g sour cream
2 tsp chipotle paste

> **Chef's tip**
> For the best results, buy real
> Mexican tortillas online – they
> have a much better flavour than
> those found in supermarkets.

Mexican street food is everywhere in LA, and I love the many different variations of tacos you can buy – pork, beef, chicken and fish in amazing sauces. The great thing about making tacos at home is that everyone can fill their own, leaving out the bits they don't like, and adding plenty of what they do. Pico de gallo, a roughly chopped salsa, doesn't usually contain avocado, but I love the creaminess it adds.

1 Sprinkle the steaks with the cumin and chilli powder. Drizzle with the olive oil and season with salt and pepper.

2 Put the sliced onions into a small bowl and cover with boiling water. Leave for 10 minutes.

3 Meanwhile, make the pico de gallo: put the tomatoes and jalapeño into a small bowl with the coriander, avocado and lime juice. Season to taste.

4 Drain the onions, then place them in a small bowl. Add the oregano, lime juice and a little salt and stir to combine.

5 Heat a large, non-stick frying pan over a high heat and cook the steaks for 3–4 minutes on each side. Transfer to a warm plate and leave to rest.

6 Heat the tortillas in a large frying pan one at a time until lightly toasted on each side.

7 Make the chipotle crema by mixing the sour cream with the chipotle paste.

8 Carve the steaks into thick slices. Place the tortillas on two plates and spoon some crema over them. Top with slices of steak, some pico de gallo and pink onions and serve straight away.

Pork Schnitzel with Celeriac Remoulade

Serves 2

2 x 220g boneless pork chops
50g plain flour
1 egg
80g fresh breadcrumbs
1 tsp dried dill
1 tsp paprika
Vegetable oil, for frying
Sea salt and freshly ground black
   pepper

For the remoulade

200g celeriac, peeled and julienned
2 tbsp mayonnaise
1 tsp wholegrain mustard
2 tbsp sour cream
1 tbsp finely chopped flat leaf parsley
Squeeze of lemon juice

To serve

2 small handfuls of watercress
Lemon wedges (optional)

Schnitzel is a real crowd pleaser in our house – I think it's the crunch of the breadcrumbs with the salty savouriness of the pork that appeals to kids and adults alike. It's quick too, as the chops are flattened before you cook them, reducing the time they spend in the pan. The remoulade is only super-fast if you have a food processor to shred the celeriac – doing it by hand will take much longer.

1 Using a sharp knife, trim the fat off each pork chop. Lay them between two pieces of cling film and use a mallet or rolling pin to flatten them out to a thickness of 5mm.

2 Put the flour into a shallow bowl, season with salt and pepper and mix well. Lightly beat the egg in a second shallow bowl. Put the breadcrumbs into a third shallow bowl and mix in the dill and paprika. Season both sides of the chops, then coat each one first in the flour, then in the egg and finally in the breadcrumbs.

3 For the remoulade, put the celeriac, mayonnaise, mustard, sour cream and parsley into a large bowl and mix well. Add a little lemon juice and season to taste. Set aside.

4 Heat a 1cm depth of vegetable oil in a frying pan. When hot, carefully add the schnitzels and cook for 2–3 minutes on each side. Drain on kitchen paper.

5 Serve the schnitzels with a generous spoonful of the remoulade, a handful of watercress and a lemon wedge (if using) on the side.

Bacon Cheeseburgers with Pickled Cucumber Burger Sauce

Serves 4

4 extra thick slices of smoked back
    bacon
1kg 20% fat minced beef
1 tbsp mild olive oil
4 slices of Monterey Jack or Cheddar
    cheese
4 burger buns with sesame seeds
1–2 tomatoes, thickly sliced
Small handful of sliced burger
    gherkins
2 large handfuls of shredded iceberg
    lettuce
Sea salt and freshly ground black
    pepper

For the burger sauce

150g mayonnaise
2 tsp Frenchy's mild American
    mustard
1 tbsp tomato ketchup
4 tbsp pickled cucumber relish
3 tsp white wine vinegar
1 tsp onion powder
1 tsp garlic powder
½ tsp sweet smoked paprika

For Americans, burger sauce is almost as important as the burgers themselves. The pickles, sauce and relish market is huge, but you can make this excellent version at home by simply mixing together a handful of ingredients that you are likely to have already in your kitchen. It is guaranteed to take your home-made burgers to the next level.

1 Preheat the grill to high.
2 Put the bacon on a baking tray and place under the grill for 8–10 minutes, or until crisp.
3 Mix together all the sauce ingredients.
4 Place the minced beef in a bowl and season with salt and pepper. Mix well with clean hands and form into 4 large burgers.
5 Heat the oil in a large frying pan and, when hot, add the burgers. Cook for 3 minutes on each side, then top each one with a slice of cheese, turn the heat down low and put a lid on the pan.
6 When the bacon is cooked, cut the burger buns in half and place under the grill until lightly toasted.
7 Spread 2 spoonfuls of the sauce on the bottom half of the buns, then put the burgers on top followed by the bacon. Now add the tomato slices, gherkins and lettuce. Spread another 2 spoonfuls of the sauce on the remaining halves of the buns and place them on top.

Veal Scallopini with Mushroom Sauce

Serves 4

15g dried porcini mushrooms
100ml boiling water
50g plain flour
4 veal escalopes (about 350g
   in total)
2 tbsp olive oil
30g butter
2 large banana shallots, peeled
   and finely diced
2 garlic cloves, peeled and finely
   chopped
150ml dry white wine
200g chestnut mushrooms, thickly
   sliced
200ml single cream
220g purple sprouting broccoli
100ml cold water
1 tbsp finely chopped flat leaf parsley
Sea salt and freshly ground black
   pepper

> **Chef's tip**
> If you have leftover wine after
> making the sauce, pour it into
> ice-cube trays and freeze for
> the next time you need a small
> quantity of alcohol to deglaze
> a pan or make a sauce.

I love cooking veal as an alternative to beef because it's very lean, extremely tender and totally delicious. As the meat is so lean and the escalopes are so thin, be careful not to overcook them – a minute on each side is all it takes. The easy sauce that goes with them is great with chestnut mushrooms, but you can swap them for Portobellini, wild mushrooms or fresh porcini, if you can get hold of them.

1 Put the dried porcini into a small, heatproof bowl and pour the boiling water over them. Cover the bowl with cling film and set aside.

2 Put the flour into a shallow dish. Season both sides of the veal with salt and pepper and coat each escalope with flour.

3 Place a large, non-stick frying pan over a medium–high heat and add the oil. When hot, add the veal, then cook for 1 minute on each side. Transfer to a plate.

4 Put the pan back on a medium heat, add the butter and, when it has melted, add the shallots and cook for 2 minutes, or until softened. Add the garlic and cook for a further 1–2 minutes before pouring in the wine. Cook on a high heat for 2 minutes, or until the liquid reduces by half.

5 Strain the mushroom liquid directly into the pan, then roughly chop the porcini. Add them to the pan with the fresh mushrooms and cream. Season to taste and reduce to a sauce consistency, then return the veal to the pan.

6 Put the broccoli into a pan with the cold water and a pinch of salt and pepper. Cook for 4–5 minutes, or until the water has evaporated and the broccoli is tender.

7 Spoon the veal and sauce onto plates and sprinkle with the parsley. Place the broccoli alongside before serving.

Sticky Pork with Asian Greens

Serves 2

2 x 300g thick pork chops
2 garlic cloves, peeled and crushed
2 tbsp hoisin sauce
1 tbsp Shaoxing rice wine
1 tbsp brown sugar
1 tbsp honey
1 tsp Chinese five-spice powder
1 tbsp vegetable oil

For the greens

1 tbsp vegetable oil
150g mangetout and/or sugarsnap
   peas
150g choi sum and/or baby pak choi
2 tbsp water
1 tbsp soy sauce
Pinch of ground white pepper

If you have more time...

... leave the chops to marinate
in the sauce for longer, as the
ingredients will meld together
beautifully and really penetrate
the pork.

This sticky Asian marinade works brilliantly with pork chops, and all the ingredients for it are great to have in the cupboard so you can easily whip up a satisfying midweek meal like this without much effort. Building a clever larder of sauces and spices is a great way to inject flavour into your meals without having to spend any extra time in the kitchen (see my advice for store-cupboard basics on pages 12–13).

1   Preheat the oven to 200°C/180°C fan/Gas 6.
2   Using a sharp knife, trim the fat off each pork chop.
3   Combine the garlic, hoisin sauce, rice wine, sugar, honey and five-spice powder in a shallow bowl. Add the pork chops and let them marinate for a few minutes.
4   Place a large, ovenproof frying pan over a medium heat. When hot, add the oil. Scrape as much marinade as possible off the chops, then put them into the pan and cook for 1–2 minutes on each side. Add the remaining marinade to the pan and place in the oven for 6–8 minutes.
5   Heat a large dry wok until smoking hot. Add the oil and stir-fry the mangetout and/or sugarsnaps for 1 minute. Add the choi sum and/or pak choi with the water, soy sauce and a pinch of white pepper. Stir-fry for another 1–2 minutes.
6   Remove the pork from the oven and serve with the stir-fried greens.

Juniper Venison Steaks with Quick-braised Red Cabbage

Serves 2

1 tsp juniper berries
2 x 200g venison steaks
1 tbsp mild olive oil
100ml port
250ml chicken stock
1 tsp thyme leaves
1 tbsp red wine jelly
25g butter
Sea salt and freshly ground black
   pepper

For the braised red cabbage
50g butter
1 small onion, peeled and finely diced
2 garlic cloves, peeled and finely
   chopped
1 tbsp soft brown sugar
1 tbsp red wine vinegar
100ml red wine
300g red cabbage, shredded
100ml chicken stock
½ tsp ground mixed spice

Chef's tip
Resting meat might seem like
a poor use of time when you're
rushing to get food on the table,
but it will make all the difference
to the end result – rested meat is
more tender and so much juicier.

Traditionally, braised red cabbage is something you cook for an hour or two to serve with your festive turkey, but red cabbage is for life, not just for Christmas! This quick-braised version takes about 15 minutes and has all the flavour of the slow-cook recipes, but with a bit more bite, as the cabbage isn't cooked for so long. It is a cracking accompaniment to venison, sausages and roast pork, as well as turkey.

1 Preheat the oven to 200°C/180°C fan/Gas 6.
2 First make the red cabbage. Place a saucepan over a medium heat and add half the butter. When it has melted, add the onion and cook for 2 minutes before adding the garlic and cooking for a further minute. Add the sugar, vinegar, wine, cabbage, chicken stock and mixed spice. Bring to a gentle simmer and cook for 10–12 minutes, or until the cabbage is tender.
3 Meanwhile, using a pestle and mortar, crush the juniper. Sprinkle over both sides of the venison, and season with salt and pepper.
4 Place an ovenproof, non-stick frying pan over a high heat. When hot, add the oil, then the venison steaks and brown for 1–2 minutes on each side, depending on their thickness. Transfer the frying pan to the oven for about 6 minutes for medium rare steaks. Place the steaks on a warm plate to rest.
5 Put the pan back on the heat, keeping a towel wrapped around the handle as it will be very hot. Deglaze the pan with the port and allow it to reduce by half.
6 Add the chicken stock and thyme and let that reduce by half too. Strain the mixture through a sieve, then pour it back into the pan. When hot, add the red wine jelly, allow it to melt, then stir in the butter. Season to taste and remove from the heat.
7 Check the cabbage, season with salt and pepper to taste, then stir in the remaining 25g butter.
8 Carve the venison into thick slices and place it on plates with the red cabbage. Spoon the port sauce over the meat to serve.

Korean-style Lamb with Sesame Cucumber

Serves 2

6 lamb rack cutlets, bone in
2 tbsp soy sauce
2 tbsp mirin
1 tbsp sesame oil
2 tbsp gochujang chilli paste
2 garlic cloves, peeled and crushed
3cm piece of fresh root ginger,
   peeled and finely grated
Shichimi togarashi (seven-spice
   powder)
   or black sesame seeds, to serve

For the sesame cucumber
1 large cucumber
2 tbsp tahini
1½ tbsp rice vinegar
1 tbsp sesame oil
1 tsp caster sugar
1 tbsp toasted sesame seeds

Gochujang sauce is a fermented chilli paste from Korea, and is hot, sweet and pungent. It is available from most of the major supermarkets and can be stirred into dipping sauces, soups, stews and fried rice (as on page 182) for a unique kick. It also makes a great marinade for meat and fish, but it's really punchy stuff, so use less if you don't like things too hot.

1   Preheat the grill to high. Line a roasting tray with foil.
2   Place a non-stick frying pan over a high heat, then place the cutlets, fat side down, for 2–3 minutes, or until the skin is golden and crisp. Remove from the pan and leave to cool.
3   Put the soy sauce, mirin, sesame oil, gochujang paste, garlic and ginger in a large bowl and mix together. Add the lamb and coat in the marinade. Place on the prepared tray and grill for 7–8 minutes, turning halfway through the cooking time.
4   Meanwhile, cut the cucumber in half lengthways and use a teaspoon to scoop out all the seeds. Cut the cucumber into thick batons about 5cm long.
5   Combine the tahini, vinegar, sesame oil and sugar in a large bowl. Add the cucumbers, then stir in the toasted sesame seeds and mix well.
6   Place the cutlets on plates and run a blowtorch over them, if you have one, until lightly charred in places. Add the cucumbers and sprinkle with a little togarashi to serve.

Mexican Beef and Jalapeño Quesadillas

Serves 4

2 tbsp olive oil, plus extra for
　brushing
1 onion, peeled and diced
2 garlic cloves, peeled and crushed
500g minced beef
2 tsp paprika
2 tsp ground cumin
1 x 400g tin of chopped tomatoes
1 x 400g tin of kidney beans, drained
　and rinsed
200g mixture of grated mozzarella
　and Cheddar cheese
4 spring onions, trimmed and sliced
80g pickled jalapeño chillies
4 x 25cm tortillas
Sea salt and freshly ground black
　pepper
Sour cream, to serve

For the salsa

4 tomatoes, diced
1 red onion, peeled and finely diced
Large handful of coriander, roughly
　chopped
Juice of 1 lime

My kids love these chilli quesadillas – they're always gone minutes after they hit the table. But my lot, especially Jack, like things particularly hot and spicy, so go easy on the jalapeños if you're feeding a more sensitive crowd, or leave them out altogether. Making the salsa from scratch might seem like an added hassle but it's definitely worth it.

1　Preheat the oven to 220°C/200°C fan/Gas 7. Line two large baking trays with baking paper.

2　Place a large, non-stick frying pan over a high heat. Add the oil and onion and cook for 2–3 minutes, or until the onion has softened. Add the garlic and cook for 2 minutes, then crumble in the minced beef. Cook over a high heat for 4–5 minutes, or until the mince is lightly browned.

3　Stir in the spices and cook for 1–2 minutes. Add the tinned tomatoes, cook for 2 minutes, then remove from the heat. Stir in the kidney beans and season to taste.

4　Lightly brush one side of a tortilla with extra oil and place on a prepared tray, oiled side down. Sprinkle a little cheese over one half and spread a quarter of the beef mixture on top. Scatter some spring onions, jalapeños and cheese on top before folding over the tortilla. Repeat for the remaining tortillas.

5　Brush one side of the 2 remaining tortillas with oil and place on top of the beef filling, oiled side up. Press them down firmly and place on the two highest shelves of the oven for 10–15 minutes, or until golden brown.

6　While the quesadillas are cooking, mix all the salsa ingredients in a bowl and season to taste.

7　Remove the quesadillas from the oven and cut into wedges before serving with a dollop of sour cream and some salsa on the side.

Minced Lamb Curry

Serves 4

2 tbsp ghee or vegetable oil

2 onions, peeled and finely chopped

5 garlic cloves, peeled and crushed

5cm piece of fresh root ginger, peeled and finely grated

1 tsp ground turmeric

3 tsp garam masala

1 tsp Kashmiri chilli powder

4 cardamom pods

2 tbsp tomato purée

500g minced lamb

500ml lamb stock

1 x 400g tin of chopped tomatoes

450g potatoes, peeled and cut into 1cm dice

1 tbsp methi (fenugreek) leaves (optional)

200g frozen peas

Small handful of fresh coriander, roughly chopped

1 green chilli, deseeded if you want a milder hit, finely sliced

Given the time-frame, a regular, slow-cooked lamb curry is out of the question, but this mince version is much quicker and no less tasty. Serve it with the Aromatic Saffron Pilaf on page 210 if time isn't an issue, or buy some naan bread or chapattis to mop up the sauce. Dried methi, or fenugreek leaves, are available from some supermarkets and specialist Indian or Middle Eastern shops, but leave them out if you can't get hold of them.

1. Place a large, non-stick sauté pan over a high heat. When hot, add the ghee or oil and the onions and cook for 5 minutes, or until lightly golden brown.
2. Add the garlic and ginger and stir for 2 minutes.
3. Reduce the heat, then add the turmeric, garam masala, chilli powder and cardamom pods and stir until aromatic.
4. Add the tomato purée and stir for a further minute.
5. Add the lamb and stir for 2–3 minutes, breaking up the meat as it cooks.
6. Add the stock and chopped tomatoes and bring to a simmer.
7. Add the potatoes and methi (if using), and cook for 10–15 minutes over a high heat, or until the sauce has thickened and the potatoes are cooked.
8. Stir in the peas and cook for 1 minute to warm through, then garnish with the coriander and chilli before serving with warm chapattis or parathas.

Pork Larb with Sticky Coconut Rice

Serves 2

2 tbsp jasmine rice

2 tbsp vegetable oil

400g minced pork

1 tsp caster sugar

2 tbsp fish sauce

1 tbsp soy sauce

Juice of 1–2 limes

2 Thai red chillies, deseeded if you want a milder hit, finely sliced

4 Thai shallots, peeled and finely sliced

4 spring onions, trimmed and finely sliced at an angle

Large handful of coriander

Large handful of mint

Round lettuce or little gem leaves, to serve

Sea salt

For the sticky coconut rice

200g jasmine rice

1 x 400g tin of coconut milk

Pinch of salt

Chef's tip

Filling the lettuce cups with the hot larb too early will make the leaves soggy, so get people to fill their own at the table.

My recent travels have taken me to the fascinating country of Laos, where the bold, aromatic food is full of fresh herbs and chilli. Larb, which roughly translates as 'meat salad', is almost the national dish, and is served with sticky rice cupped in lettuce leaves. The Laotians like their food extremely spicy, but you can reduce the number of chillies if you don't like it too hot.

1 Toast the 2 tablespoons rice for 5 minutes in a dry frying pan over a medium heat, or until golden brown. Using a pestle and mortar, grind the rice to a coarse powder.

2 For the coconut rice, put the 200g jasmine rice into a saucepan with the coconut milk and a pinch of salt. Place over a medium–high heat and bring to a simmer, then reduce the heat to low, cover with a lid and cook for 10–12 minutes.

3 Meanwhile, place a dry wok over a high heat. When it begins to smoke, add the oil, then stir-fry the pork for 2 minutes, or until it begins to brown slightly.

4 Add the sugar, fish sauce, soy sauce and lime juice and stir-fry for 5 minutes.

5 Add half the ground rice, the chillies, Thai shallots, spring onions and herbs and stir-fry for another minute.

6 Put the larb (pork mixture) into warm bowls and sprinkle with the remaining ground rice before serving with the coconut rice and lettuce leaves.

Veal Saltimbocca with Marsala Sauce

Serves 2

4 veal escalopes (about 350g
  in total)
100g taleggio cheese
8 sage leaves
4 fine slices of speck
200g fine green beans
30g plain flour
60g butter
Olive oil, for frying
120ml Marsala wine
200ml chicken stock
Sea salt and freshly ground black
  pepper

If you have more time...
... make the Decadent
Mashed Potatoes on page 213;
it goes brilliantly with the crisp
saltimbocca and rich Marsala
sauce.

This is the Union Street Café (USC) version of saltimbocca alla Romana, a classic Italian dish of veal and sage leaves covered in prosciutto. Veal is ultra-lean, so wrapping it in the ham protects the meat from drying out while it's cooking. At USC, they use lightly smoked speck to wrap the escalopes, and they slip in a piece of taleggio cheese for extra deliciousness. The Marsala sauce brings the whole thing together with a rich sweetness, creating a stunning dish in very little time.

1 Place each escalope between two pieces of cling film and gently flatten it with a meat mallet or rolling pin.

2 Cut the taleggio into 4 equal pieces and put one on each of the escalopes, followed by 2 sage leaves. Wrap the escalopes in the slices of speck and put them in the fridge for 5 minutes.

3 Meanwhile, bring a kettle of water to the boil and trim the green beans.

4 Remove the veal from the fridge and dust each one with a little flour.

5 Place two large frying pans over a high heat and, when hot, add a quarter of the butter and a little olive oil to each pan. When the butter has melted and is bubbling, place two escalopes in each pan, cheese side down, and cook for 3 minutes, or until golden and crisp.

6 Pour the boiled water into a saucepan, bring back to the boil, then cook the green beans for 3–4 minutes, or until just tender.

7 Turn the escalopes over and cook for about another 30 seconds. Transfer them to a platter and keep warm.

8 Deglaze the pans with half of the Marsala in each, then pour the wine from one pan into the other and allow it to reduce to a glaze. Add the chicken stock and reduce to a sauce consistency. Stir through the remaining butter, then season with salt and pepper to taste.

9 Serve the escalopes on warm plates with a pile of green beans and drizzle with the Marsala sauce.

Mustard and Herb Meatballs with Balsamic Glaze and Parmesan Cheese

Serves 4

100ml whole milk

2 rosemary sprigs, leaves finely chopped

5 thyme sprigs, leaves picked

150g fresh white bread (about 4 slices), crusts removed and quartered

500g minced beef

1 egg

1 tbsp Dijon mustard

Mild olive oil, for frying

125ml aged balsamic vinegar

1 x 100g bag of rocket salad

3 tbsp extra virgin olive oil

Juice of ½ lemon

20g Parmesan cheese

Sea salt and freshly ground black pepper

If you have more time...
... make the Blood Orange, Radicchio and Fennel Salad (see page 202) to go with these tasty meatballs.

There are three meatball recipes in this book (see also pages 36 and 181), and they are very different from each other, but what they have in common is that they are all very quick to make from scratch and absolutely delicious. It always pays to double the recipe so that you can put a second batch in the freezer for an instant meal in the future.

1   Pour the milk into a shallow bowl and stir in the rosemary and thyme. Add the quartered bread and allow to soak.

2   Meanwhile, put the beef, eggs and mustard into a large bowl and season with salt and pepper.

3   With clean hands, rub the soaked bread to a smooth paste between your fingers, then add it to the beef. Mix everything together until well combined. Dipping your hands in water from time to time, divide the mixture into 24 equal pieces and roll them into walnut-sized meatballs.

4   Place a large, non-stick frying pan over a medium–high heat and, when hot, add a little oil. Add the meatballs to the pan in batches and cook for 4–5 minutes, turning occasionally, until golden brown on all sides and cooked through.

5   Transfer the meatballs to a platter, then pour the oil from the pan and deglaze with the balsamic vinegar. Cook for 2–3 minutes, or until slightly reduced.

6   Meanwhile, put the rocket salad into a bowl, add the extra virgin olive oil and lemon juice and toss well.

7   Drizzle the balsamic glaze over the meatballs and grate the Parmesan over the top. Serve with the rocket salad and a crisp ciabatta loaf straight from the oven.

Rib-eye Steaks with Peppercorn Sauce

Serves 2

2 tbsp olive oil

2 x 250g rib-eye steaks

4 thyme sprigs

30g butter

1 banana shallot, peeled and finely
diced

2 tbsp green peppercorns

1 large garlic clove, peeled and finely
chopped

50ml cognac

1 tsp Dijon mustard

200ml beef stock

2 dashes of Worcestershire sauce

150ml double cream

Sea salt and freshly ground black
pepper

Chef's tip

Always dry meat and fish
thoroughly with kitchen paper
before frying, as any moisture
will slow down caramelisation,
and you risk overcooking the
steak, chop or fillet while trying
to get a nice colour.

If you have more time...

... serve with the Mustard Mash
on page 213 or the Green Beans
with Tarragon and Pine Nuts
on page 206.

Many people order steaks when they go out to
a restaurant, but they never cook them at home, which
is just daft, if you ask me. Cooking a steak is incredibly
easy – no prep, a few minutes basting with butter in
a hot pan, and a few minutes to rest afterwards, job
done. And the sauce takes only a few minutes more
to rustle up. The main thing is to buy a decent steak,
as no amount of basting or smothering with sauce
can make a rubbish steak taste anything but rubbish.

1   Place a large, non-stick frying pan over a high heat.
    Rub the olive oil over the steaks and season liberally
    with salt and pepper. When the pan is smoking hot,
    add the steaks and cook for 2–3 minutes on each
    side if you like your steaks medium rare.

2   Remove the pan from the heat, then add the thyme
    and butter, and baste, baste, baste the steaks for at
    least a minute. Turn them over and baste again. Transfer
    the steaks and thyme to a warm plate and leave to rest.

3   Return the pan to a medium heat, add the shallot and
    cook for 2–3 minutes, or until softened. Add the green
    peppercorns and garlic and cook for 1–2 minutes.

4   Pour in the cognac and flambé carefully. Add the
    mustard, beef stock and Worcestershire sauce, stir
    well and increase the heat to high. Let the stock reduce
    by half before adding the cream. Allow it to cook for
    another few minutes, or until the cream has thickened.

5   Put the rested steaks on serving plates, making sure
    to pour any resting juices into the sauce. Stir the sauce
    well and season to taste before pouring it over the
    steaks and serving with green vegetables.

Roast Pork Chops with Crushed Charlotte Potatoes and Lettuce and Apple Salad

Serves 2

1 tbsp vegetable oil
2 x 300g thick pork chops
30g butter
1 garlic clove, peeled and crushed
  with the blade of a chef's knife
2 thyme sprigs
Sea salt and freshly ground black
  pepper

For the crushed potatoes
300g Charlotte potatoes
50g smoked bacon lardons or
  pancetta
2 spring onions, trimmed and finely
  sliced

For the dressing
50ml olive oil
20ml white wine vinegar
½ tsp wholegrain mustard
Pinch of salt

For the salad
2 little gem lettuces, leaves
  separated
½ dessert apple, peeled and shaved
  with a vegetable peeler
1 tbsp finely chopped chives

Time-saving tip
Make double or triple the recipe
for this simple salad dressing
and keep it in a jar or bottle to
save time when you next need
to dress a salad.

Make sure you buy thick-cut chops for this recipe and take them out of the fridge at least five minutes before cooking, ideally longer, as bringing them nearer to room temperature will prevent the meat from drying out, which can be a real danger with pork. Dressing the potatoes while they are still warm means that they really absorb the flavours of the bacon, onions and vinaigrette, and will consequently taste much better.

1 Preheat the oven to 200°C/180°C fan/Gas 6.
2 Bring a kettle of water to the boil, then pour it into a saucepan. Season with salt and bring back to the boil over a medium–high heat. Add the potatoes and cook for 15 minutes, or until tender.
3 Place a large, ovenproof frying pan over a high heat. Drizzle the vegetable oil over the pork chops and season with salt and pepper. When the pan is hot, add the chops and cook for 1–2 minutes on each side. Add the butter and, when foaming, baste the meat with it. Add the garlic and thyme, then transfer the pan to the oven for 6–8 minutes. When the chops are cooked through, transfer to a warm plate and allow to rest.
4 Meanwhile, place a frying pan over a medium–high heat and add the bacon lardons. Cook for 5–8 minutes, or until crisp and golden. Drain on kitchen paper.
5 Combine the dressing ingredients in a bowl and whisk together.
6 When the potatoes are cooked, drain in a colander, then transfer to a bowl and crush lightly with a fork. Stir in the spring onions and crispy bacon. Drizzle over two-thirds of the dressing, then stir well and season with salt and pepper.
7 Combine the salad ingredients in a bowl, add the remaining dressing and toss well.
8 Drizzle the pork chops with some of the pan juices and serve with a generous spoonful of the crushed potatoes and the salad on the side.

Lamb Rump with Creamed Cannellini Beans

Serves 2

2 x 250g lamb rumps
2 tbsp olive oil
25g butter
200ml lamb stock
180g purple sprouting broccoli
    or fine green beans, trimmed
2 anchovies in olive oil, finely
    chopped
100ml water
Sea salt and freshly ground black
    pepper

For the creamed cannellini beans

1 tbsp olive oil
1 banana shallot, peeled and finely
    diced
2 garlic cloves, peeled and finely
    chopped
2 rosemary sprigs, leaves finely
    chopped
2 x 400g tins of cannellini beans,
    drained and rinsed
150ml double cream

This is one of those meals that punches above its weight – the deliciousness of the finished dish far outweighs the amount of effort put into creating it. The creamy, rosemary-flavoured beans are an excellent accompaniment to the lamb and purple sprouting broccoli, but you could also serve them with a juicy steak or some crisp chicken thighs, or simply on toast like posh baked beans.

1   Preheat the oven to 200°C/180°C fan/Gas 6.
2   Score the fat on the lamb with a sharp knife and season with salt and pepper. Place an ovenproof, non-stick stick frying pan over a high heat. When hot, add half the oil, then place the lamb in the pan, skin side down, and cook for 3–4 minutes on each side. Transfer the pan to the oven for 8–10 minutes.
3   Meanwhile, make the creamed cannellini. Heat the olive oil in a saucepan over a medium heat. Add the shallot and cook for 2–3 minutes, or until softened. Add the garlic and rosemary and cook for another 2 minutes. Stir in the cannellini beans and cream, then cook over a medium heat for 5 minutes. Season to taste.
4   Remove the lamb from the oven. Add the butter and baste the lamb for 2 minutes. Transfer the lamb to a warm plate to rest.
5   Replace the pan on a high heat and add the stock. Allow to boil and reduce for 5 minutes, or until the sauce thickens a little.
6   Put the broccoli into another frying pan with the remaining tablespoon of olive oil, the anchovies and water. Bring to the boil and cook for about 5 minutes. Season to taste.
7   Divide the cannellini beans and broccoli between two plates, then carve the lamb into thick slices and lay them on top. Pour the sauce over the meat before serving.

Meat-free Mains

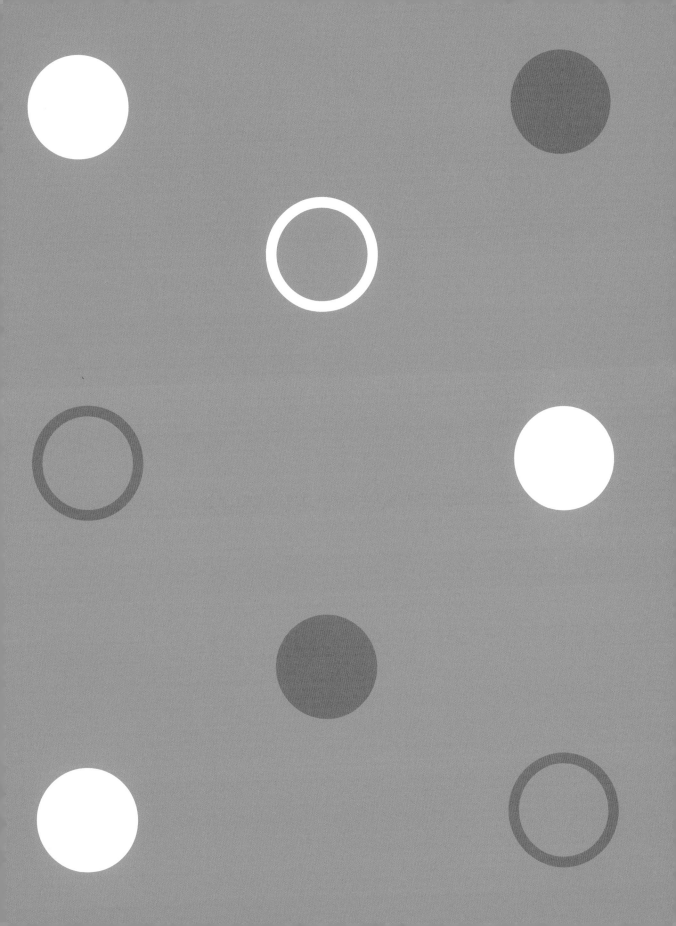

Lentil Burgers 141

Quick Butternut and Chickpea Curry 142

Truffle Mushrooms with Cheesy Polenta 145

Sichuan Sesame Noodles 146

Barbecued Mushrooms with Fennel Slaw and Onion Rings 149

Roasted Cauliflower with Israeli Couscous, Harissa Oil and Lime Crème Fraîche 150

Beetroot, Thyme and Goat's Cheese Tart with Pear and Rocket Salad 153

Vegetable Stir-fry 154

Corn and Courgette Fritters with Tomato, Avocado and Rocket Salad 157

Spicy Smoked Tofu Lettuce Cups 158

Tofu and Vegetable Laksa 161

Pea, Basil and Goat's Cheese Omelette with Shaved Asparagus and Rocket Salad 162

Lentil Burgers

Serves 4

4 tbsp olive oil

1 onion, peeled and finely chopped

2 garlic cloves, peeled and finely chopped

2 green jalapeño chillies, deseeded for a milder hit, finely chopped

1 red pepper, deseeded and diced

1 tsp ground cumin

1 tsp sweet smoked paprika

1 x 400g tin of chickpeas, drained and rinsed

1 x 250g packet of cooked Puy lentils

50g fresh breadcrumbs

30g plain flour, for dusting

4 slices of Cheddar cheese

Sea salt and freshly ground black pepper

To serve

100ml mayonnaise

2 tsp chipotle peppers in adobo sauce

1 tbsp Frenchy's mild American mustard

4 wholemeal burger buns, split open

Little gem lettuce leaves

2 large gherkins, thinly sliced lengthways

1 ripe avocado, peeled, stoned and thinly sliced

Chef's tip

To deseed a bell pepper, chop the stalk off, then stand it on the cut end and slice from top to bottom, avoiding the seeds.

In my restaurant kitchens, we have spent a lot of time trying to develop the ultimate vegan burger, and I think this is a pretty damn good one. The combination of lentils and blitzed chickpeas gives it an authentic texture, and the spiced peppers and onions give it proper depth of flavour. Leave out the cheese and sauce if you're vegan.

1   Preheat the oven to 200°C/180°C fan/Gas 6.

2   Place a non-stick frying pan over a high heat and add half the olive oil. When hot, add the onion and cook for 2–3 minutes, or until softened. Add the garlic, chillies and red pepper and cook for a further 2–3 minutes. Stir in the cumin, paprika and a big pinch of salt, then remove from the heat.

3   Put the chickpeas into a food processor and tip in the onion mixture. Pulse just until the mixture combines – you want to retain some texture. Transfer this mixture to a large bowl.

4   Add the lentils, breadcrumbs and beaten egg to the bowl, season with salt and pepper, and mix well with clean hands. Divide the mixture into 4 equal-sized burgers. Dust both sides with the flour, brushing off any excess.

5   Place a large, non-stick frying pan over a high heat and add the remaining 2 tablespoons of olive oil. When hot, add the burgers and cook for 2 minutes on each side. Transfer them to a baking tray and top each one with a slice of cheese. Place in the oven for 5 minutes. When cooked, remove from the oven and switch the grill on.

6   Meanwhile, mix together the mayonnaise, chipotle sauce and mustard.

7   Place the hamburger buns, cut side up, under the grill for 1–2 minutes, or until lightly toasted. Spread both halves with some of the mayonnaise mixture, then place the lettuce leaves on each bottom half, followed by a burger. Top with the gherkins, avocado, lettuce leaves and bun lids, and serve straight away.

Quick Butternut and Chickpea Curry

Serves 4

3 tbsp vegetable oil

1 tbsp black mustard seeds

1 tbsp cumin seeds

Small handful of curry leaves

1 large onion, peeled and finely
   chopped

500g peeled butternut squash

4 garlic cloves, peeled and crushed

3cm piece of fresh root ginger,
   peeled and finely grated

1 heaped tsp ground turmeric

1 heaped tsp paprika

2 heaped tsp ground coriander

600ml vegetable stock

1 x 400ml tin of coconut cream

2 x 400g tins of chickpeas, drained
   and rinsed

3 large handfuls of baby spinach

Sea salt and freshly ground black
   pepper

If you have more time ...

... make a double batch of the
curry, as it will taste even better
the next day.

**This straightforward, warming curry packs a hearty
punch for vegans, vegetarians and people trying
to eat less meat. It is wonderful when you first cook
it, but even better a couple of days later, as time allows
the spices to blend together and become more mellow
and rounded.**

1   Place a large non-stick saucepan over a high heat
and add the oil. When hot, add the mustard seeds,
cumin seeds and curry leaves, then stir and cook
for 30 seconds.

2   Add the onion and cook for 4–5 minutes, or until
softened and beginning to brown.

3   Meanwhile, cut the butternut squash into 1cm cubes.

4   Add the garlic and ginger to the pan and cook for
1–2 minutes.

5   Reduce the heat a little, then stir in the dried spices
and cook for 1 minute. Pour in the stock and bring
to the boil.

6   Add the squash and coconut cream, stir well, then
bring back to the boil and cook for 10–12 minutes,
or until the squash is tender and the sauce has
thickened.

7   Stir in the chickpeas, season well with salt and pepper,
then stir in the spinach. Serve the curry in warm bowls
with plain rice or the Saffron Pilaf on page 210 or some
naan bread.

Truffle Mushrooms with Cheesy Polenta

Serves 4

700g mixed mushrooms, e.g.
  chestnut, Portobello, oyster
3 tbsp olive oil
4 garlic cloves, peeled and finely
  chopped
50g porcini and truffle paste
250ml double cream
1 tbsp finely chopped tarragon
1 tbsp thyme leaves
Truffle oil, to serve

For the cheesy polenta
1.5–2 litres vegetable stock
2 rosemary sprigs, leaves finely
  chopped
200g instant/quick-cook polenta
50g Parmesan cheese, finely grated,
  plus extra to serve
100g taleggio cheese, cut into cubes
40g butter
Sea salt and freshly ground black
  pepper

Chefs often look to mushrooms when they are trying to recreate the depth of flavour that meat brings to cooking. They are full of umami and earthy notes that other vegetables simply don't have. Here the flavour of the mushrooms is intensified by stirring through some porcini and truffle paste during the cooking, and drizzling truffle oil over the top to finish.

1 Pour the stock for the polenta into a large saucepan and place over a medium heat.
2 Meanwhile, cut the various mushrooms into equal 2.5cm pieces.
3 Place a large, non-stick frying pan over a high heat and add half the oil. When hot, add half the mushrooms and fry for 2–3 minutes, or until golden brown. Drain on kitchen paper, then heat the remaining oil and fry the rest of the mushrooms. Set aside on kitchen paper.
4 Add the garlic to the pan and cook for 1 minute before adding the porcini paste, cream and herbs. Cook for 3–4 minutes over a medium heat, or until the sauce becomes very thick.
5 Meanwhile, add the rosemary to the hot stock, increase the heat and pour in the polenta. Cook for 3–5 minutes, or until tender. Stir in the Parmesan and taleggio and season to taste. Finally, stir in the butter until it has melted. Keep warm.
6 Add the mushrooms to the cream sauce and bring back to a simmer. Season to taste.
7 Serve the polenta in bowls with the mushroom sauce spooned over the top. Add a drizzle of truffle oil, a twist of black pepper and a sprinkling of Parmesan before serving.

Sichuan Sesame Noodles

Serves 4

1 onion, peeled and finely sliced

200g baby chestnut mushrooms, halved

200g oyster mushrooms, torn into equal pieces

200g mangetout, sliced in half at an angle

200g choi sum, cut into 7–8cm lengths

4 spring onions, trimmed and finely sliced at an angle

1 tbsp vegetable oil

2 tbsp sesame oil

1 tsp Sichuan peppercorns, crushed

650g ready-to-wok udon noodles

For the sesame and peanut sauce

3 tbsp tahini

2 tbsp crunchy peanut butter

4 tbsp soy sauce

4 garlic cloves, peeled and grated

5cm piece of fresh root ginger, peeled and grated

2 tbsp rice vinegar

100ml coconut milk

150ml water

To serve

½ cucumber, halved lengthways and finely sliced

4 tbsp toasted sesame seeds

Chilli oil

Sichuan pepper is a citrusy, vibrant variety of pepper from China that has a lip-tingling, mouth-numbing effect when you eat it. It elevates this simple bowl of noodles to something that packs a little more punch than your average midweek stir-fry. Udon are thick Japanese noodles that you can buy ready-cooked, but you can use whatever noodles you have in the cupboard.

1 Make the sesame and peanut sauce by combining all the ingredients for it in a bowl.

2 Prepare all the vegetables as specified for the stir-fry, and also the cucumber that will be needed to serve.

3 Place a large, non-stick wok over a high heat until it begins to smoke. Add the vegetable and sesame oils, then add the onion and peppercorns and stir-fry for 1–2 minutes. Add the mushrooms and mangetout and stir-fry for another 2 minutes.

4 Add the noodles and the sesame and peanut sauce and stir-fry for 2–3 minutes. Add the choi sum and cook for another 1–2 minutes, or until the noodles are piping hot and the sauce has reduced. Remove from the heat and stir in the spring onions.

5 Pile the stir-fry into bowls and top each with a spoonful of sesame seeds, a drizzle of chilli oil and a small handful of sliced cucumber.

Barbecued Mushrooms with Fennel Slaw and Onion Rings

Serves 2

100ml barbecue sauce
2 tsp chipotle paste
4 Portobello mushrooms, stalks
　　removed
Vegetable oil, for frying

For the fennel slaw

80g fennel, finely sliced
80g red cabbage, finely shredded
80g carrot, grated
3 tbsp mayonnaise
1 tbsp white wine vinegar
Sea salt and freshly ground black
　　pepper

For the onion rings

150g self-raising flour
1 tsp dried thyme
1 tsp garlic granules
225ml cold sparkling water
1 small onion, peeled and thickly
　　sliced into rings

If you have more time...

... cook the mushrooms on a hot barbecue with some corn on the cob to complete the feast. You can't beat the flavour that real charcoal adds.

What many vegetarians and vegans miss is the smoke and char of a barbecue, but there are some great veg that barbecue brilliantly, such as corn on the cob, asparagus, cauliflower steaks, peppers and mushrooms. The large Portobello mushrooms used here are glazed with barbecue sauce and smoky chipotle paste, then charred on a smoking hot griddle pan to bring out those barbecue flavours. Serve with the onion rings and fennel slaw for the full effect. To make this recipe vegan, use vegan mayonnaise in the slaw.

1　Preheat the oven to 200°C/180°C fan/Gas 6. Place a griddle pan over a high heat.
2　Mix the barbecue sauce and chipotle paste together in a bowl. Using a pastry brush, coat both sides of the mushrooms with the sauce mixture. Put the mushrooms on the griddle for 2–3 minutes on each side, or until they have charred lines.
3　Meanwhile, put all the vegetables for the slaw into a large bowl with the mayonnaise and vinegar. Season with salt and pepper, stir well and set aside.
4　Transfer the mushrooms to a roasting tray along with any barbecue sauce remaining in the bowl. Place in the oven for 10–12 minutes.
5　Half-fill a small pan with vegetable oil and place over a high heat.
6　Meanwhile, put the flour, thyme and garlic into a bowl and season with salt and pepper. Whisk in the sparkling water to make a batter, then add the onion rings and stir carefully to coat.
7　Once the oil has reached 180–190°C, or a drop of batter sizzles instantly, carefully add four or five onion rings at a time and cook for 2–3 minutes, or until golden brown on both sides. Drain on kitchen paper and cook the remaining rings in the same way.
8　Divide the mushrooms, coleslaw and onion rings between serving plates. Sprinkle the rings with a little extra salt before serving.

Roasted Cauliflower with Israeli Couscous, Harissa Oil and Lime Crème Fraîche

Serves 4

2 tbsp olive oil

1 tsp ground turmeric

1 cauliflower, divided into large florets

160g Israeli or pearl couscous

Large handful of mint leaves, roughly chopped

Sea salt and freshly ground black pepper

For the harissa oil

2 tbsp rose harissa

4 tbsp olive oil

For the lime crème fraîche

160g crème fraîche

Zest and juice of 1 lime

To serve

Small handful of coriander leaves

Large handful of crispy fried onions

Roasted cauliflower is nothing like the watery, slightly bitter-tasting boiled variety. It has a complex caramelised flavour that transforms it from a boring side veg into a stunning main course in its own right. Finish it with pungent harissa oil, lime crème fraîche and a handful of those incredibly moreish crispy fried onions that you can buy in supermarkets.

1 Preheat the oven to 240°C/220°C fan/Gas 9.
2 Put the olive oil and turmeric into a large bowl, season with salt and pepper and stir well to combine. Add the cauliflower and, using clean hands, toss until lightly coated in the yellow oil.
3 Tip the florets into a roasting tray and place on the top shelf of the oven for 10 minutes.
4 Meanwhile, cook the couscous according to the packet instructions. When ready, stir in the chopped mint and season with salt and pepper. Cover with a lid and put to one side until needed.
5 Combine the harissa and olive oil in a bowl and mix well. Set aside until needed.
6 Remove the tray from the oven and turn the cauliflower florets over. Return to the oven for a further 5 minutes, or until cooked through and beginning to char.
7 Combine the crème fraîche, lime zest and juice in a bowl, then taste, adding more lime juice if necessary.
8 When the cauliflower is ready, divide the florets between four plates and add a spoonful of the minted couscous and lime crème fraîche to each one. Spoon the harissa oil over the cauliflower and sprinkle with the coriander leaves and crispy fried onions before serving.

Beetroot, Thyme and Goat's Cheese Tart with Pear and Rocket Salad

Serves 4

2 x 320g sheets of ready-rolled puff
pastry
250g cream cheese
150g red onion chutney
400g cooked beetroot
2 tsp thyme leaves
1 tsp nigella seeds
120g soft goat's cheese
1 tbsp runny honey
1 egg, lightly beaten
Sea salt and freshly ground black
pepper

For the pear and rocket salad
50g shelled walnuts
120g rocket leaves
1 small ripe pear, cored and sliced
3 tbsp extra virgin olive oil
1½ tbsp white balsamic vinegar

Ready-made pastry is a brilliant thing to have in the fridge or freezer for quick tarts like this one. Yes, it's possible to make your own puff pastry, but it will take you two hours or so, and shop-bought, all-butter puff is pretty good these days. Once you have tried this beetroot and goat's cheese version, follow the same general method but with different toppings, such as marinated tomatoes, sautéed mushrooms or caramelised onions.

1 Preheat the oven to 220°C/200°C fan/Gas 7. Line two baking trays with baking paper.
2 Place the walnuts in a separate small baking tray and toast in the oven for 5 minutes. Set aside until needed.
3 Using a sharp knife and a 22cm round plate or bowl, cut a circle out of each pastry sheet. Place the circles on the prepared sheets and prick the middle of each several times with a fork.
4 Mix the cream cheese and onion chutney together, then spread half the mixture over each circle, leaving a 2cm border.
5 Using a mandolin, cut the beetroot into thin slices. Arrange them over the chutney in slightly overlapping circles.
6 Sprinkle with the thyme leaves, nigella seeds and chunks of goat's cheese, drizzle with the honey and season with salt and pepper. Brush the edges of the pastry with the beaten egg, then place in the oven on the two highest shelves for 15–20 minutes, or until golden and crisp.
7 Meanwhile, put the rocket and pear into a large bowl and season with salt and pepper. Whisk together the oil and vinegar, then pour over the salad and mix well. Roughly chop the walnuts and scatter them over the salad.
8 Remove the tarts from the oven and cut into wedges. Serve with the rocket salad on the side.

Vegetable Stir-fry

Serves 2

1 carrot, halved lengthways and
  sliced at an angle
150g baby corn, cut in half at an
  angle
1 yellow courgette, halved
  lengthways and sliced at an angle
2 garlic cloves, peeled and finely
  chopped
3cm piece of fresh root ginger,
  peeled and grated
150g pak choi, sliced
150g asparagus, trimmed and cut
  into 2.5cm pieces at an angle
200g oyster mushrooms
2 spring onions, trimmed and finely
  sliced at an angle
1 tbsp vegetable oil
1 tbsp sesame oil
2 tbsp soy sauce
2 tbsp oyster sauce
1 tbsp honey
1 tsp cornflour
Cooked rice, to serve

Time-saving tip
Rather than snapping off the
woody parts of asparagus one
by one, use a chef's knife to cut
them off in one fell swoop while
they are still bunched in the
elastic band.

Making a stir-fry is a quick, hot business, and this veg-only version should take around five minutes from start to finish. Any longer than this and the veg will be overcooked and unappetising, so get all the prep done before you start and you will be ready to add each of the vegetables as and when you need to. Speed is definitely of the essence, so measure out all the oils and sauces in advance too.

1 Prepare all the vegetables before you start cooking. Place a wok over a high heat until smoking hot. Add the oils, then stir-fry the carrot and corn for 1–2 minutes.

2 Add the courgette, garlic and ginger and stir-fry for 2 minutes before adding the pak choi, asparagus and oyster mushrooms. Pour in the soy sauce, oyster sauce and honey and stir-fry for another 1–2 minutes.

3 Mix the cornflour with 3 tablespoons water, add to the wok and stir well. Add the spring onions and serve immediately with rice.

Corn and Courgette Fritters with Tomato, Avocado and Rocket Salad

Serves 4

2 corn on the cob
2 tbsp olive oil, plus extra for frying
4 spring onions, trimmed and finely sliced
1 green chilli, deseeded if you want a milder hit, finely chopped
2 eggs, separated
100ml whole milk
200g courgettes, grated
80g self-raising flour
Small handful of fresh basil, chopped
100g mixture of Cheddar and mozzarella cheese, grated
50g feta cheese, crumbled
Zest of 1 lemon
Sea salt and freshly ground black pepper

For the salad
200g baby plum tomatoes, halved
100g rocket leaves
1 ripe avocado, peeled, stoned and sliced
1 tbsp white balsamic vinegar
2 tbsp extra virgin olive oil

Relaxed, tasty foods, like these sweetcorn and courgette fritters, are ideal for a brunch or weekend lunch. Stripping the corn from the cobs might seem like a hassle, but raw corn will colour and char far more than the wet-from-the-tin variety. If you're really pressed for time, of course you can used tinned, unsweetened corn, but make sure you drain and dry it thoroughly so it doesn't add any water to the batter.

1 Preheat the oven to 140°C/120°C fan/Gas 1.
2 Remove the corn kernels from the cobs by standing each cob upright and running a sharp knife down the sides.
3 Place a large, non-stick frying pan over a high heat. When hot, add the oil and corn and cook for 2–3 minutes, or until the corn begins to char lightly. Add the spring onions and chilli and cook for a further 2 minutes. Remove from the heat and leave to cool slightly.
4 Put the egg yolks and milk into a bowl. Put the egg whites into a separate bowl and whisk until firm peaks form.
5 Squeeze any excess liquid from the courgette and add it to the egg yolks along with the cooked corn mixture. Add the flour, basil, cheeses and lemon zest. Season with salt and pepper, stir well, then gently fold in the egg whites.
6 Place two large, non-stick frying pans over a medium–high heat and pour a thin layer of olive oil into each one. When hot, place two large, separate spoonfuls of the corn mixture in each pan. Cook for 2 minutes on each side, or until golden and crisp. When ready, carefully transfer the fritters to a baking tray and place in the oven to keep warm. Cook the remaining mixture in the same way.
7 Put all the salad ingredients into a bowl and mix well. Serve the hot corn fritters with a little salad on the side.

Spicy Smoked Tofu Lettuce Cups

Serves 2

2 tbsp vegetable oil

1 tbsp sesame oil

1 onion, peeled and diced

4 garlic cloves, peeled and crushed

250g baby corn, thickly sliced

250g Portobello mushrooms, diced

2 tbsp Shaoxing rice wine

400g smoked tofu, crumbled

80g water chestnuts, roughly
   chopped

3 tbsp soy sauce

2 tbsp sriracha chilli sauce

1 tbsp rice vinegar

2 large handfuls of beansprouts

Large handful of coriander, roughly
   chopped

To serve

2 iceberg or round lettuce leaves,
   or 4 little gem leaves

1 red chilli, deseeded if you want
   a milder hit, finely sliced

Handful of crispy fried onions

Chef's tip

Don't put the tofu mixture into
the lettuce cups too soon or the
leaves will become too soggy
to lift to your mouth.

Crumbled smoked tofu is a brilliant starting point for many vegan dishes – it has a great texture for scrambles, stir-fries and salads and the smoky flavour adds a depth that can sometimes be lacking in vegan food. Add some aromatics, some Asian veg and this great combination of Chinese flavours and you have a winning meat-free main course in under 30 minutes.

1 Place a large, non-stick wok over a high heat. When smoking hot, add the oils, then the onion and stir-fry for 1–2 minutes. Add the garlic and baby corn and stir-fry for 1–2 minutes. Add the mushrooms and rice wine and stir-fry for another 2 minutes.

2 Sprinkle the tofu into the pan and stir in the water chestnuts. Add the soy sauce, sriracha and rice vinegar and stir-fry for 1–2 minutes before adding the beansprouts. Stir-fry for a further minute, remove from the heat, then stir in the coriander.

3 Serve the tofu mixture in bowls with the lettuce leaves on the side. Sprinkle with the red chilli and crispy onions before serving.

Tofu and Vegetable Laksa

Serves 4

120g Malaysian laksa paste
1 tbsp sriracha chilli sauce
2 tbsp soy sauce
600ml vegetable stock
1 x 400ml tin of coconut milk
250ml coconut cream
2 tsp lemongrass paste
2 tbsp fish sauce (omit for
    vegetarians)
200–300g medium egg noodles
100g baby chestnut mushrooms,
    halved
200g baby courgettes, thickly sliced
    at an angle
200g fried tofu puffs, cut in half
200g mangetout
1 x 225g tin of bamboo shoots,
    drained
Juice of 1 lime
2 large handfuls of beansprouts

To serve
Sliced red chilli, deseeded for a
    milder hit
Fresh coriander

Unlike regular tofu, which is dense and quite difficult to infuse with flavour, the fried tofu puffs used here are like absorbent pillows that take in all the lovely spiciness of the broth. You can buy tofu puffs from Asian supermarkets and specialist websites, but if you can't get hold of any, shallow fry some cubes of smoked tofu until crispy, then add them to the saucepan at the very end.

1 Make the broth by putting the laksa paste, sriracha, soy sauce, vegetable stock, coconut milk, coconut cream, lemongrass paste and fish sauce (if using) into a saucepan and placing it over a medium heat.

2 Bring a kettle of water to the boil, then pour it into a second saucepan and return to the boil. Add the noodles and cook according to the packet instructions, until tender. Drain well and divide them between four serving bowls.

3 Once the broth is simmering, add the mushrooms and courgettes to it and cook for 2 minutes. Add the tofu puffs, mangetout and bamboo shoots and cook for another 2 minutes.

4 Taste the broth and add some lime juice to taste.

5 Ladle the broth and vegetables into the bowls containing the noodles. Add a small handful of beansprouts to each bowl and serve garnished with the red chilli and coriander.

Pea, Basil and Goat's Cheese Omelette with Shaved Asparagus and Rocket Salad

Serves 4

200g frozen peas
20g butter
Small handful of basil leaves, roughly chopped
8 large eggs, beaten
150g goat's cheese log, thickly sliced
20g Parmesan cheese, grated
Sea salt and freshly ground black pepper

For the salad

250g asparagus, trimmed
Large handful of rocket leaves
Juice of ½ lemon
3 tbsp olive oil

A basic omelette has to be the ultimate single-ingredient fast food because it can be on the plate within a couple of minutes of cracking the first egg. This pea, basil and goat's cheese version shouldn't take that much longer, but it is worth exercising a little patience when it goes under the grill – a bit of colour on the goat's cheese will make the whole thing really sing.

1 Preheat the grill to high.
2 Put the peas into a colander and hold them under running tepid water for about a minute. This will defrost them without cooking them.
3 Place a large, ovenproof frying pan over a medium-high heat and add the butter. When hot, add the peas, shake the pan and cook for 1–2 minutes.
4 Add the basil and stir well before pouring in the beaten eggs, then cook for 2–3 minutes, or until the omelette is beginning to set on the bottom.
5 Meanwhile, prepare the salad. Using a mandolin or vegetable peeler, slice the asparagus lengthways into very fine shavings and place them in a bowl with the rocket. Whisk the lemon juice, olive oil and a pinch of salt in a small bowl, then pour this dressing over the salad and toss well.
6 Dot the goat's cheese slices over the omelette, sprinkle with the Parmesan and season with salt and pepper. Place the frying pan under the grill for 1–2 minutes, or until the eggs are set on top and the goat's cheese has begun to brown.
7 Transfer the omelette to a board or plate, slice into wedges and serve with the asparagus and rocket salad.

Pasta,
Rice
and
Grains

Cacio e Pepe with Parmesan Crisps 169

Tomato, Mascarpone and Pancetta Rigatoni 170

Linguine Vongole with Nduja and Cherry Tomatoes 173

Crab and Courgette Spaghetti 174

Farfalle with Brown Butter, Peas and Sage 177

Porcini Tagliatelle with Pine Nuts 178

Saffron Orzo with Turkey Meatballs 181

Korean-style Prawn Fried Rice 182

Chicken Biryani 185

Spanish Chorizo Rice 186

Lentil and Bulgur Tabbouleh with Grilled Feta 189

Crispy Chicken, Quinoa and Cauliflower 'Couscous' with Charred Corn 190

Cacio e Pepe with Parmesan Crisps

Serves 2

60g Parmesan cheese, finely grated
200g bucatini
1½ tsp black peppercorns
100g butter
20g pecorino cheese, finely grated
Sea salt

In several Italian dialects *cacio e pepe* translates as 'cheese and pepper', and that's essentially all that goes into this sauce. The magic ingredient that binds them together is the pasta cooking water. It is full of starch, which emulsifies with the butter and helps the sauce cling to the pasta. The Parmesan crisps are optional, but such an easy and impressive way to finish the dish.

1   Preheat the oven to 200°C/180°C fan/Gas 6. Line a baking tray with baking paper.

2   To make the crisps, take half the Parmesan and place it in four equal piles on the prepared tray. Place on a high shelf in the oven for 10–12 minutes, or until the Parmesan has turned golden brown. Set aside.

3   Bring a kettle of water to the boil. Half-fill a saucepan with it, season with salt and return to the boil. (It's important to add just enough water to cover the pasta so that the water will become as starchy as possible.) Add the pasta, stir well and cook for 10 minutes, or until al dente.

4   Meanwhile, toast the peppercorns in a dry frying pan until aromatic. Using a pestle and mortar, grind them coarsely.

5   Place a large sauté pan over a medium heat and melt the butter in it. Add the ground pepper and let the butter foam, then add a ladleful of the pasta water and bring to the boil. Swirl the pan or whisk the contents to emulsify the sauce.

6   Remove the pasta from the water with tongs and add it to the sauté pan with a second ladleful of the water and the remaining Parmesan. Stir well to coat, and add more pasta water if needed.

7   Add the pecorino and salt, tossing the pan to combine.

8   Serve in bowls with the Parmesan crisps crumbled over the top.

Tomato, Mascarpone and Pancetta Rigatoni

Serves 4

3 tbsp olive oil

250g diced pancetta or smoked bacon

1 large onion, peeled and finely diced

3 garlic cloves, peeled and finely chopped

1 tsp Italian seasoning

100g sunblush tomatoes, roughly chopped

1 x 400g tin of chopped tomatoes

200ml chicken stock

200g mascarpone cheese

400g rigatoni

20g Parmesan cheese, finely grated, plus extra to serve

Small handful of basil leaves, roughly chopped

Sea salt and freshly ground black pepper

Time-saving tip

Buy a packet of diced pancetta or bacon lardons and store it in the fridge (for up to a month) as a useful standby. It's so handy for rustling up carbonara or other pasta sauces like this one at the last minute.

Here we have a tasty midweek supper that uses lots of store-cupboard and fridge ingredients that have a relatively long shelf life – tinned tomatoes, pancetta, mascarpone – making it a top standby recipe to feed your hungry family. If you leave out the pancetta and switch the chicken stock for vegetable bouillon or water, this becomes a really tasty, meat-free pasta sauce or base for pizza or vegetarian lasagne.

1. Place a large sauté pan over a medium–high heat and add the oil. When hot, add the pancetta and cook for 3–4 minutes, or until crisp and golden. Remove a big spoonful from the pan and drain on kitchen paper, then put to one side to use as garnish.

2. Add the onion to the pan and cook until softened, then add the garlic and cook for 2 minutes.

3. Stir in the Italian seasoning, both lots of tomatoes, the chicken stock and mascarpone. Bring to a gentle simmer and cook for 10 minutes, or until slightly thickened.

4. Meanwhile, bring a kettle of water to the boil. Pour into a saucepan, season with salt and return to the boil. Add the pasta, then stir and cook for 10 minutes, or until al dente. Drain the pasta, reserving the water.

5. Add the pasta to the sauce and stir well to coat. Add a ladleful of the pasta water, if needed. Season to taste, then add the Parmesan and basil and stir again.

6. Serve in warm bowls and sprinkle with the reserved pancetta and a little more Parmesan.

Linguine Vongole with Nduja and Cherry Tomatoes

Serves 4

200ml dry white wine

1.5kg clams, rinsed and any closed ones discarded

3 tbsp olive oil

2 banana shallots, peeled and finely diced

6 garlic cloves, peeled and finely sliced

80g nduja sausage

250g baby plum tomatoes, halved

400g linguine

2 small handfuls of flat leaf parsley, finely chopped, plus extra to serve

Sea salt and freshly ground black pepper

Nduja is a soft, spreadable salami from the Calabria region of Italy, and is seriously hot and spicy. It is usually spread on toast or served with cheese, but can also be stirred through pasta sauces, scrambled eggs, soups and stews to add colour and warmth. Shellfish, such as clams, love a bit of heat, but the sweetness of the tomatoes keeps this dish from being over the top.

1 Place a saucepan that has a tight-fitting lid over a high heat until smoking hot. Meanwhile, line a colander with muslin or a new J-cloth and sit it over another pan.

2 Pour the wine into the smoking pan, add the clams, then cover with the lid and cook for 3–4 minutes, until the clams have opened. Strain through the prepared colander.

3 Place a large sauté pan over a medium heat, add the olive oil and shallots and cook for 2 minutes. Add the garlic and cook for a further 2 minutes.

4 Increase the heat, add the nduja and break it up with a spoon. Cook for another 2 minutes, then pour in the clam liquor and cook for 5 minutes, before adding the tomatoes.

5 Bring a kettle of water to the boil, then pour it into a saucepan, season with salt and return to the boil. Add the pasta and cook for 10 minutes, or until al dente.

6 While the sauce is simmering and the pasta is cooking, pick the meat from all but a dozen or so of the clams.

7 When the pasta is ready, drain in a colander, reserving the cooking water. Add the pasta to the sauce along with a ladleful of the reserved water, the clam meat and the parsley. Toss the pan well in order to coat the pasta with the sauce.

8 Season to taste, then serve in warm bowls, garnished with the clams in their shells and some extra parsley.

Crab and Courgette Spaghetti

Serves 2

200g spaghetti

2 tbsp olive oil

1 banana shallot, peeled and finely chopped

3 garlic cloves, peeled and finely sliced

1 long red chilli, deseeded if you want a milder hit, finely chopped

50ml dry white wine

300g courgettes, grated or julienned

50g brown crab meat

100g crème fraîche

150g white crab meat

Zest of 1 lemon

2 tbsp roughly chopped dill

40g butter, cubed

Sea salt and freshly ground black pepper

Gone are the days when you would have to cook a live crab to make this pasta sauce; happily, you can now buy ready-picked brown and white crab meat from fishmongers and supermarkets, which saves you the bother. It is expensive because it can only be done by hand, but worth it to be able to cook this lovely, light summer dish in half an hour. Don't cook the crab for long or it will lose some of its gentle flavours.

1 Bring a kettle of water to the boil. Pour into a saucepan, season with salt and return to the boil. Add the pasta and cook for 10 minutes, or until al dente.

2 Meanwhile, place a large, non-stick sauté pan over a medium–high heat and add the oil. When hot, add the shallot and cook for 2 minutes.

3 Add the garlic and chilli and cook for a further 2 minutes. Pour in the white wine, then increase the heat to high and cook until the wine reduces by half.

4 Add the courgettes, brown crab meat and crème fraîche and stir well.

5 Drain the spaghetti, reserving the water. Add the pasta to the sauté pan along with half a ladleful of the cooking water, the white crab meat, lemon zest, half the dill and the butter and cook for 1 minute. Toss the pasta to ensure it is well coated with the sauce and season to taste.

6 Serve in bowls, sprinkled with the remaining dill.

Farfalle with Brown Butter, Peas and Sage

Serves 4

400g farfalle
250g fresh peas
80g Parmesan cheese, grated,
  plus extra to serve
Sea salt and freshly ground black
  pepper

For the brown butter

200g butter
Large handful of sage leaves
3 garlic cloves, peeled and finely
  chopped

Chef's tip

Get into the habit of always putting a bowl under the colander when draining pasta so you never pour the starchy cooking water down the plughole – you always need a little to help the sauce really stick to the pasta.

Despite being a really quick recipe, this is a deeply delicious pasta sauce. Browning, or burning, the butter completely transforms the flavour into something much richer and more interesting. Hold your nerve during the browning, and don't take the pan off the heat until you smell the tell-tale aroma – it should be sweet and nutty with rich caramel notes.

1 Bring a kettle of water to the boil. Half-fill a saucepan with it, season with salt and return to the boil. (It's important to add just enough water to cover the pasta so that the water will become as starchy as possible.) Add the pasta, stir well and cook for 10 minutes, or until al dente.

2 Meanwhile, put the butter into a sauté pan and place it over a high heat. When it begins to brown, remove from the heat, add the sage leaves and garlic and stir well.

3 Drain the pasta, reserving the cooking water.

4 Pour a ladleful of the reserved water into the sauté pan and add the peas. Return the pan to the heat and cook for 1–2 minutes, stirring constantly.

5 Add the pasta and Parmesan and stir well. Add a little more pasta water, if needed, and season to taste.

6 Serve in warm bowls with a twist of black pepper and extra Parmesan sprinkled on top.

Porcini Tagliatelle with Pine Nuts

Serves 2

15g dried porcini mushrooms

200g tagliatelle

30g pine nuts

1 tbsp olive oil

60g butter

1 banana shallot, peeled and finely chopped

2 garlic cloves, peeled and finely chopped

100ml dry white wine

200g fresh mushrooms, ideally porcini or wild ones, finely sliced

2 tbsp finely chopped tarragon

25g Parmesan cheese, finely grated, plus extra to serve

1 tbsp flat leaf parsley, roughly chopped

3 tbsp crème fraîche

Sea salt and freshly ground black pepper

You can use any variety of mushrooms for this sauce, as each type will bring something different to the finished dish. Try a wild mushroom mixture, or use fresh porcini when they are in season during the autumn. Always include the dried porcini, though – rehydrating them in boiling water creates an instant mushroom stock that is packed with flavour and gives the sauce a real boost.

1 Bring a kettle of water to the boil. Put the dried porcini into a small, heatproof bowl and add enough boiling water to cover them. Cover with cling film and set aside.

2 Pour the remaining boiling water into a saucepan, add some salt and return to the boil. Add the pasta and cook for 7–10 minutes, or until al dente.

3 Meanwhile, put the pine nuts into a dry frying pan and place over a medium heat, shaking the pan until they are lightly toasted. Set aside until needed.

4 Put the olive oil and half the butter into a sauté pan and place over a low heat. When the butter has melted, add the shallot and cook gently for 2–3 minutes. Add the garlic and cook gently for another 2 minutes.

5 Increase the heat to high, add the white wine and let it reduce by half.

6 Strain the liquid from the soaked porcini directly into the pan, then roughly chop the hydrated mushrooms and add them too. When the liquid has reduced by half, add the fresh mushrooms and tarragon and stir well until the mushrooms have softened.

7 Drain the pasta, reserving the water. Add the pasta to the mushroom mixture, then stir in the Parmesan, parsley and remaining butter, plus some of the reserved water, if needed.

8 Season the pasta to taste, stir in the crème fraîche and serve in bowls, sprinkled with extra Parmesan and the pine nuts.

Saffron Orzo with Turkey Meatballs

Serves 4

500g minced turkey thigh meat

40g Parmesan cheese, finely grated, plus extra to serve

3 tbsp flat leaf parsley, finely chopped

Zest of 1 lemon

1 egg, lightly beaten

50g fresh breadcrumbs

50g plain flour

1 tbsp olive oil

220ml chicken stock

Sea salt and freshly ground black pepper

For the saffron orzo

80g butter

2 banana shallots, peeled and finely diced

2 garlic cloves, peeled and finely chopped

Pinch of ground saffron

1 litre chicken stock

400g orzo

2 tbsp finely chopped oregano leaves

20g Parmesan cheese, finely grated

When you're keen to get dinner on the table in half an hour, risotto is out of the question; it simply takes too long for the rice to reach that ideal creamy texture. Orzo, however, cooks in 10 minutes and is equally velvety and comforting. When it comes to the meatballs, always buy minced turkey thigh meat – it will be much more flavourful than the breast and juicier too.

1 Put the minced turkey, Parmesan, parsley, lemon zest, egg and breadcrumbs into a large bowl and season with salt and pepper. Mix well and divide into 24 walnut-sized meatballs. Place in the fridge until needed.

2 To make the orzo, melt half the butter in a large sauté pan over a medium heat. Add the shallots and cook for 2 minutes, then add the garlic and cook for a further 2 minutes.

3 Add the saffron and litre of stock and bring to the boil. Pour in the orzo and cook for 10 minutes, or until al dente, stirring occasionally.

4 Remove the meatballs from the fridge and lightly coat each one in the flour. Place a large, non-stick frying pan over a high heat. When hot, pour in the olive oil, add the meatballs and cook until golden brown all over.

5 Pour the 220ml stock into the pan, bring to a simmer and cook the meatballs gently for a further 5 minutes, or until cooked through and the sauce has thickened.

6 When the orzo is ready, stir in the oregano, then add the Parmesan and remaining 40g butter. Season to taste and serve in warm bowls with the turkey meatballs and some extra Parmesan on top.

Korean-style Prawn Fried Rice

Serves 4

2 eggs, lightly beaten
2 tbsp vegetable oil
2 tbsp sesame oil
400g peeled raw tiger prawns,
    cut in half lengthways
2 tbsp gochujang chilli paste
3 x 250g packets of ready-cooked
    long grain and wild rice
2 tbsp soy sauce
1 tbsp fish sauce
2 large handfuls of beansprouts
150g frozen peas
Sea salt and ground white pepper

To serve

100g kimchi, roughly chopped
1 tsp black sesame seeds
Large handful of crispy fried onions
    (available from supermarkets)
4 spring onions, trimmed and finely
    sliced at an angle
Sriracha chilli sauce

> **If you have more time...**
> ... and are feeling indulgent, fry
> some eggs and place them on
> top of the rice before garnishing.
> The runny yolk seeping into the
> rice is amazing.

The Korean gochujang chilli paste stirred through this fried rice gives it a lovely colour and a great kick, while the kimchi gives it the sour, fermented flavour that is associated with Korean food. Of course, fried rice is only a quick option if you have leftover or ready-cooked rice, as it has to be completely cold when stir-fried, or it will be soggy and disappointing.

1   Place a large, non-stick wok over a high heat. Season the eggs with salt and white pepper.
2   Add half of the two oils to the pan, swirl around to coat, then pour in the eggs. Cook for 1 minute, stirring gently to break them into pieces, then slide them onto a plate.
3   Return the wok to a high heat. When hot, add the remaining oils, then the prawns, and stir-fry for 1–2 minutes. Add the gochujang paste and stir well.
4   Add the rice, soy sauce and fish sauce and stir-fry for another 2–3 minutes. Return the eggs to the pan, add the beansprouts and peas, then stir-fry for a further 2–3 minutes.
5   Serve the rice in warm bowls, garnished with the kimchi, sesame seeds, crispy fried onions, spring onions and a drizzle of sriracha.

Chicken Biryani

Serves 4

2 tbsp vegetable oil

1 onion, peeled and diced

1 large carrot, peeled and diced

2 garlic cloves, peeled and crushed

3cm piece of fresh root ginger,
   peeled and grated

2 tbsp Madras curry paste

350g boneless chicken thighs,
   cut into 2cm cubes

2 ripe tomatoes, diced

350g basmati rice

700ml chicken stock

2 large handfuls of baby spinach

2 large handfuls of fresh coriander

120g fresh or frozen peas

Sea salt and freshly ground black
   pepper

Poppadoms, to serve

For the minted yoghurt

1½ tsp ground cumin

300g natural yoghurt

Small handful of fresh mint,
   finely chopped

Biryani is a firm family favourite in our house, being mildly spiced but still full of flavour and nicely filling. In India, biryani is traditionally a layered dish, but this all-in-together version is quick, light and just as tasty. We always make our own curry pastes in the restaurants, but a good-quality ready-made version is a speedy shortcut that won't compromise the end result in any way.

1   Place a large, non-stick saucepan over a medium–high heat and add the oil. When hot, add the onion and cook for 2–3 minutes. Add the carrot and cook for 2 minutes.

2   Stir in the garlic and ginger, then add the curry paste and cook for 1–2 minutes.

3   Add the chicken, stir well, then add the tomatoes, rice, stock and seasoning. Stir again and bring to a simmer. Cover and cook over a low heat for 10 minutes.

4   Meanwhile, prepare the minted yoghurt. Put the cumin into a small frying pan over a high heat and stir until roasted and aromatic. Transfer to a small bowl, add the yoghurt and mint, season with salt and pepper and mix well.

5   Roughly chop the spinach and coriander, then add them to the chicken pan together with the peas. Stir well and cook for a further 2–3 minutes.

6   Serve the curry in bowls with the minted yoghurt and poppadoms alongside.

Spanish Chorizo Rice

Serves 4

280g spicy cooking chorizo
   sausages
2 tbsp olive oil
1 red onion, peeled and finely diced
1 large green pepper, deseeded
   and diced
2 garlic cloves, peeled and finely
   sliced
1 tsp hot smoked paprika
1 tsp ground cumin
2 tbsp tomato purée
200g cherry tomatoes, halved
Pinch of ground saffron
300ml chicken stock
200g cooked piquillo peppers
3 x 250g packets of cooked long-
   grain rice
1 x 400g tin of black beans, drained
   and rinsed
100g pitted green olives
Sea salt and freshly ground black
   pepper

To serve
Small handful of flat leaf parsley,
   roughly chopped
30g manchego cheese, shaved
   (optional)

The paprika-flavoured oil from the chorizo permeates this cracking rice dish, making it rich, sumptuous and very moreish. When I don't have time to make an authentic paella from scratch, I cheat and use ready-cooked long-grain rice. This has a different texture from the short-grain Bomba rice traditionally used in paella, but it carries the flavours beautifully.

1 Place a large sauté pan over a medium heat. Cut the chorizo into thick slices, then add to the pan with the olive oil. Cook for 5 minutes, or until browned and crispy on both sides. Transfer to a plate.

2 Add the onion to the pan and cook in the chorizo fat for 2–3 minutes, or until softened. Add the green pepper and garlic and cook for 2 minutes.

3 Add the paprika, cumin and tomato purée and stir for 1 minute. Add the tomatoes, saffron and stock and bring to a simmer.

4 Cut the piquillo peppers into thick slices and add to the pan along with the rice, black beans and olives. Cook for 4–5 minutes.

5 Season with salt and pepper and sprinkle with the parsley and manchego (if using) before serving.

Lentil and Bulgur Tabbouleh with Grilled Feta

Serves 4

250g bulgur wheat
4 pieces of feta cheese, roughly 70g each
1 tbsp olive oil
250g mini cucumbers, thickly sliced
2 celery sticks, finely chopped
1 red onion, peeled and finely diced
200g cherry tomatoes, halved
2 large handfuls of mint, roughly chopped
100g flat leaf parsley, roughly chopped
2 x 250g packets of cooked Puy lentils
Sea salt and freshly ground black pepper

For the dressing
60ml extra virgin olive oil
3 tbsp pomegranate molasses
2 tbsp red wine vinegar
¼ tsp ground allspice

To serve
120g pomegranate seeds
Lemon wedges

When you grill feta, it doesn't melt – it just becomes softer and creamier with deliciously crisp edges. It's amazing with this lentil-filled tabbouleh, as the salty, tangy cheese is tempered by the sweet and sticky pomegranate molasses in the dressing. You can serve the salad on its own or as part of a big summer lunch, perhaps with the Blood Orange, Radicchio and Fennel Salad on page 202 and the Warm Aubergine, Tomato and Burrata salad on page 31.

1   Preheat the grill. Line a baking tray with a silicone mat.
2   Bring a kettle of water to the boil. Put the bulgur into a small saucepan, cover generously with the boiled water, then bring to the boil over a high heat. Cook for 7–10 minutes, or until the bulgur has softened.
3   Tip the cooked bulgur into a sieve and hold it under running cold water until cool. Drain well and set aside.
4   While the bulgur is cooking, place the feta on the prepared tray, drizzle with the olive oil and season with salt and pepper. Cook under the grill for 10–12 minutes, or until it has browned well.
5   Meanwhile, prepare all the vegetables and herbs as listed and put them into a large bowl with the lentils and bulgur.
6   Whisk together all the dressing ingredients, then pour over the bulgur mixture and stir well. Season to taste.
7   Remove the feta from the grill and check that it is well coloured. If any parts haven't browned properly, run a blowtorch over them, or return to the grill for a few more minutes.
8   Divide the bulgur between four plates and place a piece of feta on top. Sprinkle with the pomegranate seeds and put a lemon wedge on to each plate before serving.

Crispy Chicken, Quinoa and Cauliflower 'Couscous' with Charred Corn

Serves 4

500g boneless chicken thighs, cut into strips 1cm thick
2 tbsp chipotle paste
1 tsp dried oregano
Vegetable oil, for frying
40g plain flour
40g cornflour
Sea salt and freshly ground black pepper
Lime wedges, to serve

For the quinoa and cauliflower 'couscous'

2 corn on the cob
2 tbsp olive oil
1 red onion, peeled and diced
350g cauliflower, grated
250g broccoli, finely chopped (including stems)
250g cooked quinoa
150g roasted red peppers, from a jar, thickly sliced
1 x 400g tin of kidney beans, drained and rinsed
2 large handfuls of fresh coriander, roughly chopped

For the dressing

50ml extra virgin olive oil
2 tsp wholegrain mustard
1 tbsp agave syrup
Juice of 2 limes

Time-saving tip

You can buy ready-grated cauliflower from the supermarket.

This brilliant, colourful salad is great with the crispy chicken, but would be equally good with fried smoked tofu, grilled halloumi or feta. It's packed with superfoods, such as quinoa, kidney beans and raw broccoli, so it's extremely good for you, as well as being very tasty and satisfying. Make double the batch and feel virtuous as you take it to work for lunch the next day.

1   Put the chicken, chipotle paste and oregano into a bowl. Season with salt and pepper and mix well.

2   For the 'couscous', remove the corn kernels from the cobs by standing each cob upright and running a sharp knife down the sides.

3   Place a large frying pan over a high heat and add the olive oil. When hot, fry the corn until lightly charred.

4   Add the onion and cook for 1–2 minutes. Add the cauliflower and cook for a further 2–3 minutes.

5   Remove the pan from the heat and stir in the broccoli, quinoa, red pepper, kidney beans, coriander and shredded lettuce. Transfer to a bowl and put to one side.

6   Place a shallow sauté pan over a high heat and add a 1cm depth of oil. Combine the flour and cornflour in a bowl, then lightly coat each piece of chicken in the mixture. Add to the hot oil in batches and cook until crisp outside with no sign of pink inside. When ready, drain on kitchen paper.

7   Meanwhile, whisk together the dressing ingredients and season with salt and pepper. Pour over the 'couscous' and mix well. Spoon onto plates, top with the crispy fried chicken and serve with wedges of lime.

Dips
and
Sides

Pea and Mint Guacamole 197

Black Houmous with Pitta Crisps 198

Anchovy Tapenade with Ciabatta Toasts 201

Blood Orange, Radicchio and Fennel Salad 202

Moroccan Carrot Salad 205

Green Beans with Tarragon and Pine Nuts 206

Courgette Fries 209

Aromatic Saffron Pilaf 210

Decadent Mashed Potatoes with Three Variations 213

Pea and Mint Guacamole

Serves 4

175g frozen peas
1 tbsp olive oil
1 small onion, peeled and finely
   sliced
2 ripe avocados
Juice of 2 limes
3 mint sprigs, leaves picked
Sea salt and freshly ground black
   pepper

Time-saving tip
To peel avocados quickly and
with minimal waste, cut them
in half around the stone, then
slip a dessertspoon between
the flesh and the skin and run
it gently around the fruit, keeping
the back of the spoon as close
to the skin as possible. The flesh
should pop out easily, leaving
very little behind.

This dip is seriously green! It's so much brighter,
fresher and better for you than shop-bought guacamole,
and is really quick and simple to make. It's a great
standby recipe too, as chances are that you already
have all the ingredients in the kitchen. It is great with
crunchy vegetables, such as radishes, baby carrots,
sugarsnap peas, baby gem lettuce leaves and mini
cucumbers, but also with tortilla chips or spread
on toast as an alternative to houmous.

1   Put the peas into a colander and hold under running
    tepid water for about a minute to defrost them.
2   Place a frying pan over a medium heat and add the oil.
    When hot, sweat the onion for 3–4 minutes, or until
    soft, stirring regularly to prevent it catching.
3   Slice the avocados in half, remove the stones and scoop
    out the flesh with a spoon. Chop the flesh and put it
    into a blender or mixing bowl with the lime juice and
    mint leaves.
4   Add the peas to the onions in the frying pan and allow
    to warm through for a minute.
5   Tip the onions and peas into the blender or bowl and
    season with salt and pepper. Pulse or mash with a fork
    just until the mixture combines – you want to retain
    some texture. Taste and adjust the seasoning as
    necessary. Serve with a selection of crunchy
    vegetables or nacho chips.

Black Houmous with Pitta Crisps

Serves 4

4 pitta breads
120ml olive oil, plus extra for
    drizzling
1 x 400g tin of chickpeas, drained
    and rinsed
100g black sesame paste
1 garlic clove, peeled and crushed
1 rosemary sprig, leaves finely
    chopped
Juice of 1–2 lemons
Sea salt

Swapping regular tahini for black sesame paste in this houmous transforms the colour but also subtly changes the taste, as black sesame seeds are less sweet than the lighter, cream-coloured ones, and have an earthy nuttiness that goes brilliantly with the rosemary and garlic in this dip. Black sesame paste can be found in Asian supermarkets as it's a staple in Japanese cooking, where they often sweeten it with honey and use it in pastries, puddings and ice cream. However, it's also really delicious just spread on toast.

1   Preheat the oven to 200°C/180°C fan/Gas 6.
2   Cut each pitta bread into 8 triangles. Split open each triangle and separate the halves, removing any bready dough that is attached. Arrange the triangles in a single layer on two baking trays, then drizzle with olive oil and sprinkle with sea salt before placing in the oven for 3–4 minutes.
3   Put the chickpeas, sesame paste, garlic, rosemary, 2 tablespoons olive oil and the juice from one lemon into a food processor. Season with salt and blend until you have a smooth paste. Taste the houmous and add more olive oil, lemon juice and salt as necessary.
4   Take the pitta crisps out of the oven and turn them over, removing the thinner ones that have already crisped up. Return the trays to the oven for another 2–3 minutes, or until all the remaining triangles are golden brown and crunchy.
5   Transfer the houmous to a bowl and drizzle with a little olive oil before serving with the pitta crisps.

Anchovy Tapenade with Ciabatta Toasts

Serves 4–6

½ ciabatta loaf

3–4 tbsp olive oil, plus extra
for drizzling

1 x 100g jar of good-quality
anchovies in olive oil

2 garlic cloves, peeled and crushed

1 banana shallot, peeled and finely
diced

Small handful of parsley leaves

125g pitted Kalamata olives

2 tsp red wine vinegar

Sea salt and freshly ground black
pepper

Take two classics of Mediterranean cooking, anchovies and olives, blitz them together with a good-quality extra virgin olive oil and you have a punchy dip or an intense topping for bruschette in under 20 minutes. Serve with crunchy veg or lightly toasted bread and a chilled bottle of white wine and be instantly transported to a terrace in the south of France.

1 Preheat the grill to high.

2 Slice the ciabatta very finely into 8–10 slices, then drizzle with olive oil on each side and lay them on a baking tray. Place under the grill and toast for 2–3 minutes on each side, or until golden brown and crisp. Beware – the thinner the bread, the quicker it will burn, so check often.

3 Meanwhile, drain the anchovies, reserving any oil. Put the fish into a food processor with the garlic, shallot, parsley and olives and blitz to a purée.

4 Add the red wine vinegar and season with salt and pepper, then, with the motor running, pour in any reserved anchovy oil, followed by the measured olive oil until you reach the desired consistency.

5 Taste and adjust the seasoning as necessary, then serve with the crisp ciabatta toasts and crudités.

Blood Orange, Radicchio and Fennel Salad

Serves 4

1 fennel bulb
3 blood oranges
1 head of radicchio, or a mixture
    of different varieties, such as
    Trevisano or Castelfranco

For the dressing
3 tbsp white balsamic vinegar
1 tsp honey
1 tsp wholegrain mustard
Juice of ½ blood orange
Juice of ½ lemon
2 tbsp chopped dill
4 tbsp extra virgin olive oil
Sea salt and freshly ground black
    pepper

Try to get your hands on a few different varieties of radicchio for this salad, such as the pale, red-splattered leaves of Castelfranco, the curly fingers of Trevisano Tardivo, or the classic Chioggia, to make it even more of a visual feast. It looks stunning with the blood oranges and sliced fennel, and makes a beautiful addition to a big lunch. Serve with chicken, fish or barbecued meats, or turn it into a starter by placing a couple of burratas on top. If you can't get radicchio, red chicory will work just as well flavour-wise.

1 Trim the fennel, cut it into quarters, then slice it very finely using a mandolin.
2 Using a sharp knife, peel the oranges, being careful to remove all the pith. Finely slice the flesh into discs.
3 Remove the core from the radicchio and tear the leaves into bite-sized pieces. Put these into a large salad bowl and add the fennel and blood orange slices.
4 Combine all the dressing ingredients in a bowl, season with salt and pepper and whisk well. Taste and, if necessary, add more acidity or sweetness.
5 Pour half the dressing into the salad bowl and mix carefully with your hands until everything is coated. Drizzle the remaining dressing over the top before serving.

Moroccan Carrot Salad

Serves 4

500g carrots
2 tbsp rose harissa
1 tbsp finely chopped preserved
    lemon
1 green chilli, deseeded and finely
    sliced
2 garlic cloves, peeled and crushed
Juice of 1 lemon
1 tsp ground cumin
2 tbsp olive oil
Large handful of coriander leaves,
    roughly chopped
Sea salt and freshly ground black
    pepper

Time-saving tip
To save more time, don't peel the carrots – a lot of the goodness is just under the skin and gets lost by peeling, so give them a brisk scrub instead.

I recently visited Morocco to film a TV show, and I fell in love with all the North African flavours, including harissa, preserved lemon, cinnamon, cumin and rose water. This stunning dressing works brilliantly with other ingredients too, so make a double batch and keep it in the fridge to drizzle over some grilled halloumi or roasted cauliflower, or to stir through a big bowl of couscous. Alternatively, drizzle some extra olive oil over the top and serve it as a dip with flatbreads and baby veg.

1   Bring a kettle of water to the boil, then pour it into a saucepan and place over a medium heat.

2   Peel the carrots and cut them into thin rounds. Add them to the boiling water, bring to the boil again, then drain immediately. Transfer the carrots to a bowl of iced water to stop them cooking.

3   Meanwhile, put the harissa, preserved lemon, chilli, garlic, lemon juice, cumin and olive oil into a small saucepan and place it over a medium heat for 2–3 minutes to warm through and combine.

4   Drain the carrots thoroughly and transfer them to a serving dish. Spoon over the dressing and stir well. Season with salt and pepper, then sprinkle with the chopped coriander and stir again before serving.

Green Beans with Tarragon and Pine Nuts

Serves 4

20g pine nuts
350g fine green beans, trimmed
25g butter
2–3 tarragon sprigs, leaves roughly
  chopped
Sea salt

Time-saving tip

Toast more pine nuts than you need and keep the excess in an airtight jar to speed things up next time you need to scatter them over a salad or pasta dish, such as Porcini Tagliatelle (see page 178).

This is a great way to make green beans more interesting without having to do very much. Suddenly a boring side dish has a bit more to say for itself! It makes a cracking accompaniment to grilled fish, roast chicken and barbecued lamb or pork chops, or you could swap the butter for a light vinaigrette and serve it as a salad as part of a summer lunch.

1 Bring a kettle of water to the boil, then pour it into a saucepan and bring to the boil with the lid on.
2 Place a small frying pan over a medium heat and add the pine nuts in a single layer. Toast for about 4 minutes, shaking the pan from time to time, particularly towards the end of the cooking time.
3 Add the green beans to the boiling water and cook for 2–3 minutes, or until cooked but still crisp.
4 Drain the beans and return them to the empty pan. Add the butter and, with the lid on, shake the pan a couple of times until the butter has melted and coated the beans.
5 Tip the beans into a serving dish, mix in the tarragon leaves and sprinkle over the toasted pine nuts. Season with salt before serving.

Courgette Fries

Serves 4

3 medium courgettes
Pinch of saffron
100ml water
1 litre flavourless oil, e.g. groundnut,
    for frying
190g semolina
60g '00' flour
Sea salt
Dried marjoram, to serve

Chef's tip
If you don't have a cooking thermometer, the oil is ready (180°C) when a cube of bread added to it browns in 30 seconds.

We serve these crispy courgette fries in Union Street Café in London, where they are hugely popular with people just ordering a drink after work. They also go really well with burgers (see pages 111 and 141), grilled chicken and fish. Alternatively, just scatter some crumbled feta over the fries to make a meal of them. Be warned – they are very moreish!

1 Finely julienne the courgettes with a mandolin or julienne peeler and put them into a large bowl.
2 Season the courgettes with plenty of salt to release the water.
3 Using a pestle and mortar, grind the saffron to a powder and sprinkle it over the courgettes. Add the water, stir well and set aside for 10–15 minutes.
4 Meanwhile, pour the oil into a large heavy-based saucepan and place over a medium–high heat.
5 Mix the semolina and flour together in a large bowl.
6 Once the oil has reached 180°C, lift a handful of the courgettes from the water and toss them in the flour mixture until lightly coated. Fry them in the hot oil until golden and crisp. Using a slotted spoon, transfer them to a plate lined with kitchen paper. Repeat this step with the remaining courgettes.
7 Transfer the fries to a serving bowl and season with salt and the marjoram before serving.

Aromatic Saffron Pilaf

Serves 4

50g ghee or butter
1 large onion, finely sliced
400g basmati rice
Pinch of saffron
Small handful of curry leaves
800ml chicken stock
1 cinnamon stick
5 cardamom pods
5 cloves
1 tsp sea salt

A spiced pilaf is such a versatile dish and makes a great addition to curry night. Try it with the Malaysian Fish and Okra Curry on page 59, or the Minced Lamb Curry on page 123. Get all the prep done up front and you won't have to worry about time – you can just get on with cooking the main event. It will make your kitchen smell heavenly in the meantime.

1 Place a non-stick saucepan over a high heat and add the ghee (or butter). When hot, add the onion and cook for 5–8 minutes, stirring occasionally.

2 Meanwhile, put the rice into a large bowl and cover with water. Swirl it around with your hand, then pour out the water. Refill the bowl and repeat until the water is clear. Drain and set aside.

3 Using a pestle and mortar, grind the saffron to a powder.

4 Add the curry leaves to the onion and cook for 1 minute. Now add the saffron, chicken stock, cinnamon stick, cardamom pods, cloves, salt and rice. Stir well and cover with a lid. Bring to the boil, then immediately reduce the heat to low. Allow to cook for 12–15 minutes, then turn the heat off and leave to sit for 2–3 minutes before serving.

Decadent Mashed Potatoes with Three Variations

Serves 4

1kg Yukon Gold or Désirée potatoes, peeled and cut into 1cm cubes
75g butter
100ml whole milk
100ml double cream
Sea salt and freshly ground black pepper

Variation 1: Mustard Mash

1 tsp English mustard
1 tbsp Dijon mustard
2 tsp wholegrain mustard

Variation 2: Truffle Mash

30g porcini and truffle paste
30ml white truffle oil

Variation 3: Garlic and Herb Mash

2 garlic cloves, peeled and crushed
2 tbsp woody herbs, e.g. rosemary, thyme, sage, leaves finely chopped
2 tbsp soft herbs, e.g. parsley, chives, dill, finely chopped

Chef's tip

The hotter the potato when you put it through the ricer, the fluffier the mash, so move fast once the potatoes have been drained.

Mashed potatoes are a great accompaniment for so many dishes, but these three decadent options are almost worthy of top billing. Pair them with a rib-eye steak, some good-quality sausages or a robust fillet of white fish and you have simple, fast food without any fuss. Investing in a potato ricer will make mashing the potatoes much easier and quicker, and the results are so much smoother than with a conventional masher. Once you've tried one, you'll never look back.

1   Bring a pan of salted water to the boil. Add the potatoes and cook for 15 minutes with the lid on.

2   Meanwhile, if you're making the regular, mustard or truffle mash, put the butter, milk and cream into a small saucepan and bring to a gentle simmer. For the mustard mash, add the mustards to the warm cream mixture. For the truffle mash, add the truffle paste and truffle oil to the pan instead.

3   For the garlic and herb mash, heat the butter in a small saucepan, add the garlic and woody herbs, and cook for 2–3 minutes. Pour in the milk and cream and bring to a gentle simmer. Add the soft herbs and cook for another 2–3 minutes.

4   When the potatoes are cooked, drain in a colander. Put them through a potato ricer as quickly as possible and return them to the saucepan.

5   Pour over the flavoured cream and mix well. Season to taste with salt and pepper, stir again and serve.

Puddings

Burnt Meringue with Poached Rhubarb 219

Mango, White Chocolate and Passion Fruit Parfaits 220

Spiced Peach, Apple and Almond Crumble 223

Pain Perdu with Summer Fruit Compote 224

Banana Split with Salted Caramel Chocolate Sauce 227

Cheat's Cheesecake with Macerated Strawberries 228

Fig Tarts with Vanilla and Honey Mascarpone 231

Rhubarb and Ginger Cheesecake Pots 232

Cinnamon Ice Cream Sandwiches with Winter Fruit Compote 235

Calvados Toffee Apple Pancakes 236

Choc Nut Vegan Mousse 239

Flourless Chocolate and Raspberry Pots 240

Dark Chocolate and Coffee Mousse 243

Tiramisu Pots 244

Burnt Meringue with Poached Rhubarb

Serves 4

350g rhubarb, cut into 5cm lengths
30ml grenadine liqueur
Zest and juice of ½ orange
Seeds from 1 vanilla pod
30g caster sugar
30ml water
150g strawberries, thickly sliced
Crème fraîche, to serve

For the pistachio crumble
30g butter
30g plain flour
30g caster sugar
30g nibbed pistachios

For the meringue
3 large egg whites
100g caster sugar

The secret to perfect, crisp meringues is cooking them at a low temperature really, really slowly, which rules them out for this book. However, the soft meringues here are cooked at the last minute with a blowtorch, bringing a lovely dark caramel flavour to the finished dish. The result is a restaurant-quality dessert that is still produced within 30 minutes.

1   Preheat the oven to 180°C/160°C fan/Gas 4. Line a small baking tray with baking paper.
2   Start by making the pistachio crumble: put the butter, flour and sugar into a food processor and pulse until the mixture resembles breadcrumbs. Add the pistachios and pulse just a couple of times, until the nuts are roughly chopped. Pour the mixture into the prepared tray and place in the oven for 10–15 minutes, or until lightly golden.
3   Meanwhile, put the rhubarb into a small saucepan with the grenadine, orange zest and juice, vanilla seeds, sugar and water. Place over a high heat, cover with a lid and cook for 3–4 minutes, until the rhubarb is tender but still holding its shape. Using a slotted spoon, transfer the rhubarb to a bowl.
4   Return the pan to the hob and heat the liquid until it reduces to a thick syrup. Leave to cool slightly, then fold in the strawberries, followed by the rhubarb.
5   Remove the crumble from the oven and leave to cool.
6   To make the meringue, put the egg whites into a large bowl and beat with an electric whisk until soft peaks form. Gradually add the caster sugar, 2 tablespoons at a time, until it is all incorporated and firm peaks have formed.
7   Smear a spoonful of the meringue onto each plate. Place the remainder in a piping bag and pipe a few meringue 'kisses' on each plate. Run a blowtorch over the meringue until golden and burnt in places.
8   Spoon some rhubarb mixture onto each plate. Drizzle over the syrup, then add a spoonful of crème fraîche. Finally, break up the pistachio crumble and sprinkle over the top before serving.

Mango, White Chocolate and Passion Fruit Parfaits

Serves 4

30g coconut flakes
250g ripe mango flesh
40ml passion fruit pulp
  (about 2 fruits)
Zest of ½ lime
Juice of 1 lime

For the mousse

70ml coconut milk
125g white mini marshmallows
200g white chocolate chips
250ml double cream
1 tsp vanilla paste
100ml passion fruit pulp
  (about 5–6 fruits)

Time-saving tip

Make sure you create space in your freezer before you start, as you will need it for chilling the white chocolate and the mousse.

When time is short, it is difficult to produce a fancy layered dessert with lots of different elements, as you have to wait for each layer to set before adding another. A parfait in a glass or bowl, however, is a great way to pull it off, and this white chocolate version with mango, passion fruit and coconut is exquisite.

1 Place four serving glasses in the freezer to chill.

2 To make the mousse, put the coconut milk and marshmallows into a small saucepan, place over a medium heat and stir until the marshmallows have melted. Place the white chocolate in a small heatproof bowl, pour in the marshmallow mixture and stir until the chocolate has melted. Pour this mixture into a shallow tray and put straight into the freezer to cool down quickly.

3 Whip the double cream and vanilla paste with an electric whisk until stiff peaks form. Fold the 100ml passion fruit pulp into the cream.

4 Remove the white chocolate from the freezer and make sure it's cool. Transfer to a mixing bowl, add a spoonful of the cream and whisk until well combined. Gently fold in the rest of the cream until combined.

5 Remove the glasses from the freezer and spoon the mousse into them. Return them to the freezer for 10 minutes.

6 Meanwhile, toast the coconut flakes in a small frying pan until golden brown. Set aside to cool.

7 Chop the mango into 1cm dice and mix with the passion fruit pulp, lime zest and juice.

8 Spoon the mango mixture into the glasses and sprinkle with the toasted coconut before serving.

Spiced Peach, Apple and Almond Crumble

Serves 6

500g tinned peach slices (about
   2 x 415g tins, drained)
500g peeled and diced Bramley
   apple (about 3 fruits)
3 tbsp marmalade
1 tsp ground mixed spice
30g soft light brown sugar
100g soft amaretti biscuits, crumbled
100ml orange juice
50ml almond liqueur
Whipped cream, crème fraîche
   or ice cream, to serve

For the almond crumble

100g plain flour
100g cold butter, diced
80g golden caster sugar
1 tsp almond extract
40g flaked almonds, roughly
   chopped
40g rolled oats

Chef's tip

Make this crumble in advance,
then put it into the oven when
you sit down to your main course.
It will be bubbling and golden
brown by the time you are ready
for pudding.

Using good-quality tinned peaches not only means you avoid having to prep any fresh fruit, but also that you can enjoy this fragrant spiced crumble all year round. The combination of sweet peaches, tart apples and distinct almond flavour (think Bakewell tarts) is a knock-out, and certain to be a crowd pleaser whatever time of year you rustle it up.

1   Preheat the oven to 240°C/220°C fan/Gas 9.
2   Place the peaches and apple in a shallow ovenproof dish. Stir in the marmalade and mixed spice. Sprinkle over the brown sugar and amaretti, then pour in the orange juice and almond liqueur.
3   To make the crumble, put the flour, butter and sugar into a bowl and quickly rub together until the mixture resembles breadcrumbs. Add the remaining ingredients and mix well. Sprinkle the crumble over the fruit.
4   Place the dish on the top shelf of the oven for 15–20 minutes, or until the apples are tender and the crumble topping is golden brown.
5   Serve with unsweetened whipped cream, crème fraîche or ice cream.

Pain Perdu with Summer Fruit Compote

Serves 4

1 x 400g brioche loaf
2 large eggs
100ml whole milk
100ml double cream
Seeds from 1 vanilla pod
½ tsp ground cinnamon
½ tsp ground cardamom
2 tbsp caster sugar, plus extra
   for sprinkling
1 tbsp vegetable oil
60g butter
Crème fraîche, to serve

For the compote

2 tbsp crème de cassis liqueur
50g caster sugar
180g strawberries, thickly sliced
100g raspberries
100g blueberries

Chef's tip

The pain perdu can also be
served with the Winter Fruit
Compote on page 235,
depending on the time of year
and what fruits are in season.

Pain perdu is basically posh eggy bread, and this lightly spiced version is made even more elegant by being served with a simple compote of summer fruits. If possible, use slightly old brioche for this, as it absorbs more of the egg and cream mixture, and the finished result will be crisper round the edges. You will need a blowtorch to caramelise the sugar at the end, but if you don't have one, simply dust the whole dish with icing sugar for a little extra sophistication.

1 Cut the brioche into large slices about 10 x 5cm, trimming off any excess crust.

2 Put the eggs into a bowl with the milk, cream, vanilla seeds, cinnamon, cardamom and sugar and whisk together. Pour into a shallow dish.

3 Put the crème de cassis and caster sugar for the compote into a small sauté pan over a high heat and reduce to a thick syrup. Set aside.

4 Meanwhile, dip the brioche slices in the egg mixture for just 30 seconds each, turning them so that both sides are evenly coated.

5 Put the vegetable oil and butter into a large, non-stick frying pan over a medium–high heat. When the butter has melted, carefully add the brioche slices and cook until golden brown on both sides.

6 Add the berries to the syrup and stir together gently.

7 Sprinkle the sugar evenly on the presentation side of each brioche slice, then run a blowtorch over it until the sugar melts and turns golden brown.

8 To serve, place a slice of brioche on each plate, adding a spoonful of the compote and a dollop of crème fraîche on the side.

Banana Split with Salted Caramel Chocolate Sauce

Serves 2

30g pecan or macadamia nuts, or a mixture of both
1 tbsp caster sugar
2 ripe bananas, peeled halved lengthways
4 scoops of vanilla ice cream, to serve

For the sauce
50g dark muscovado sugar
20g butter
85ml double cream
30g dark chocolate chips
½ tsp sea salt

My kids love an old-school banana split, which has to be one of the quickest ever puddings to put together. This salted caramel version is not tricky or too time-consuming, but it takes this nursery favourite to a new level. Caramelising the bananas brings out all the sophisticated flavours of vanilla, honey and rum in the fruit, while the salted caramel in the chocolate sauce keeps the whole dish from being too sweet.

1   Preheat the oven to 200°C/180°C fan/Gas 6.
2   Start by making the sauce: put the muscovado sugar, butter, cream and salt into a small saucepan and place over a medium heat. Stir well and bring to a gentle simmer, then cook for 1 minute. Leave to cool for 1 minute.
3   Place the chocolate chips in a small heatproof bowl and pour the caramel over them. Stir until the chocolate has melted and the sauce is well combined, then leave to cool.
4   Put the nuts on a baking tray and place in the oven for 5 minutes, or until lightly toasted. Allow to cool before roughly chopping them.
5   Sprinkle the caster sugar over the cut side of the bananas, then run a blowtorch over each one to caramelise it well. Alternatively, place the bananas, sugar side up, under a hot grill for 5 minutes, or until caramelised.
6   Place two halves of banana on each serving plate, then put 2 scoops of ice cream in the middle. Drizzle the caramel sauce over the top and sprinkle with the toasted nuts before serving.

Cheat's Cheesecake with Macerated Strawberries

Serves 4

200g cream cheese
3 tbsp icing sugar
Squeeze of lemon juice
Seeds from ½ vanilla pod
300ml double cream
4 digestive biscuits
3 tbsp caster sugar
50g unsalted butter
1 tbsp mint leaves, to garnish

For the macerated strawberries
200g strawberries, quartered
2 tbsp icing sugar
100ml Sauternes, Muscat or other
   sweet wine

Chef's tip
If you are feeding children, leave
out the sweet wine, or replace
it with lemon juice or balsamic
vinegar for a little added
sharpness.

Everyone loves a cheesecake, but the baking of the base and the setting of the cream cheese mean that it isn't the quickest pudding to whip up. This upside-down version, however, has all the elements of a traditional cheesecake, but with no hanging around. Macerating strawberries, which involves just sprinkling them with sugar and setting them aside, is a brilliant chef's trick for bringing out the sweetness in the fruit; it takes seconds to do, but the results are incredible.

1 Line four ramekin dishes with cling film and place them in the freezer to chill.

2 To macerate the strawberries, put them into a bowl with the icing sugar and wine. Stir well, then cover with cling film and set aside for 15–20 minutes.

3 Put the cream cheese and icing sugar into a bowl. Add the lemon juice and vanilla seeds and mix together until smooth.

4 Pour the cream into a second bowl and whisk into soft peaks, then fold it into the cream cheese mixture.

5 Remove the chilled ramekins from the freezer and fill with the cream cheese mixture, levelling the surface with a palette knife or spatula. Place in the fridge until required.

6 Put the biscuits into a food processor and pulse into coarse crumbs. Alternatively, place them in a plastic bag and crush with a rolling pin.

7 Place a non-stick saucepan over a medium heat and add the caster sugar. Once it has melted and begun to caramelise, carefully add the butter and gently shake the pan to combine it with the caramel as it melts.

8 Add the biscuit crumbs and shake the pan to coat them in the caramel. Pour the mixture onto a plate and place in the fridge for 5 minutes. When cool, crumble into pieces.

9 Remove the ramekins from the fridge and turn out the cheesecakes onto plates, discarding the cling film. Spoon the strawberries over and around the cheesecakes and sprinkle the biscuit 'base' over the top. Garnish with a little fresh mint before serving.

Fig Tarts with Vanilla and Honey Mascarpone

Serves 4

1 x 320g sheet of ready-rolled
    all-butter puff pastry
6 ripe figs, thickly sliced
¼ tsp ground cinnamon
1 egg, lightly beaten
1 tbsp demerara sugar

For the vanilla and honey
mascarpone
150g mascarpone cheese
2 tbsp honey, plus extra for drizzling
Seeds from 1 vanilla pod
Zest of ½ lemon

These tarts are so quick and easy to make that you really have no excuse for buying in dessert. Ripe figs with cinnamon is a gorgeous combination, but you can try this recipe with most fruits as they come into season – strawberries, blueberries, mango and blackberries would all be delicious. The vanilla and honey mascarpone is an irresistible addition, but vanilla ice cream or crème fraîche would also be good if time is tight.

1   Preheat the oven to 220°C/200°C fan/Gas 7. Line a baking tray with baking paper.
2   Unroll the pastry and cut off a widthways strip about 7cm wide (you can freeze this for decorating future pies). Cut the remaining pastry into 4 equal rectangles. Place them on the prepared tray, spacing them apart, then prick all over with a fork, leaving a 1cm border around the edge.
3   Arrange the fig slices on top, slightly overlapping them in places, but keeping them inside the borders.
4   Sprinkle the cinnamon over the figs and brush the borders with the beaten egg. Sprinkle the entire surface of the tarts with the sugar, then place in the oven on a high shelf for 12–15 minutes, or until the pastry is golden and crisp.
5   Meanwhile, place all the mascarpone ingredients in a small bowl and whisk together until smooth.
6   Remove the tarts from the oven and transfer to plates. Place a spoonful of the mascarpone beside each tart, then drizzle with a little extra honey before serving.

Rhubarb and Ginger Cheesecake Pots

Serves 4

300g rhubarb, trimmed and cut
   into 2cm pieces
30g stem ginger, finely chopped
2 tbsp stem ginger syrup
30ml grenadine liqueur
2 tbsp caster sugar
120g gingernut biscuits

For the cheesecake mixture
200g double cream
200g cream cheese
150g Greek yoghurt
Zest of ½ lemon
1 tbsp vanilla extract
5 tbsp caster sugar
2 tbsp orange liqueur

Here is another way to make a quick cheesecake (see page 228 for an upside-down version with macerated strawberries). It has a no-bake ginger biscuit base and is made in individual glasses, so the cream cheese layer doesn't need to set before serving. You can eat it as soon as you make it, or keep it in the fridge until needed.

1 Put the rhubarb, stem ginger, stem ginger syrup, grenadine and sugar into a non-stick saucepan. Place over a medium heat and cook for 4–5 minutes, stirring occasionally, until the rhubarb begins to soften around the edges. Pour the mixture into a shallow tray and place in the fridge to cool.

2 To make the cheesecake mixture, pour the cream into a bowl and whisk until soft peaks form. Place the remaining cheesecake ingredients in a separate bowl and whisk until combined. Fold in the cream.

3 Put the biscuits in a food processor and pulse into fine crumbs. Alternatively, place them in a plastic bag and crush with a rolling pin.

4 Divide the crumbs between four serving glasses, then spoon in the cheesecake filling.

5 Remove the rhubarb topping from the fridge and spoon it into the glasses. Serve immediately, or keep in the fridge until needed.

Cinnamon Ice Cream Sandwiches with Winter Fruit Compote

Serves 4

1 x 320g sheet of ready-rolled
  all-butter puff pastry
25g soft light brown sugar
2 tsp ground cinnamon
40g butter, softened
4 large scoops of vanilla ice cream,
  to serve

For the compote

100g peeled and diced Granny Smith
  apple (about 1 fruit)
100g peeled and diced pear
  (about 1 fruit)
75g soft light brown sugar
100ml red wine
½ tsp ground mixed spice
Zest and juice of ½ orange
80g blackberries

Here is a clever way to transform a scoop of vanilla ice cream into something much more impressive with very little effort. The cinnamon pastry discs add spice and crunch, while the apple and blackberry compote provides a warming and sharp contrast. You can make the discs and the compote in advance, so it's just a case of putting all the elements together at the last minute.

1   Preheat the oven to 220°C/200°C fan/Gas 7. Line a baking tray with baking paper.

2   Cut the pastry in half lengthways so that you end up with two 13 x 23cm rectangles. Place one rectangle on the prepared tray and place the other in the freezer for future use in another recipe.

3   Combine the sugar and cinnamon in a small bowl. Spread the butter evenly over the chilled pastry. Sprinkle the cinnamon sugar all over the butter and pat with a spoon to make sure it's well stuck down. With the narrower edge towards you, roll up the pastry tightly to form a thick roll, then place it in the freezer for 5 minutes to firm up.

4   Meanwhile, put all the compote ingredients, apart from the blackberries, into a small saucepan. Place over a high heat and cook for 4–5 minutes.

5   Remove the cinnamon roll from the freezer and cut it into 8 slices about 1.5cm thick. Line two baking trays with baking paper and place 4 slices of cinnamon roll on each tray, spacing them well apart. Pat each one down lightly with your fingers. Place a sheet of baking paper over each tray of rolls, then sit another baking tray on top to weigh them down lightly. Place in the oven for 10 minutes. (If you don't have four baking trays, bake the rolls in batches.)

6   Add the blackberries to the compote and cook for another 2–3 minutes. Set aside to cool slightly.

7   Remove the rolls from the oven and lift off the top trays and paper. Set aside to cool.

8   When you are ready to serve, place a cinnamon roll on each plate. Top with a scoop of ice cream and place another cinnamon roll on top. Serve with a big spoonful of warm compote on the side.

Calvados Toffee Apple Pancakes

Serves 4

30g pecan nuts
350g green apples
100g butter
50ml Calvados
½ tsp vanilla paste
80g dark muscovado sugar
100ml double cream
Vanilla ice cream, to serve

For the pancake batter

150g plain flour
1½ tsp baking powder
2 tbsp caster sugar
1 large egg
150ml whole milk
30g butter, melted
Pinch of salt

As children, we all love toffee apples, but when was the last time you ate one as an adult? Inspired by this nostalgic flavour combination, these apples in caramel have been given a grown-up makeover by adding a touch of Calvados, or apple brandy, to the caramel, making it a little bit more sophisticated and utterly delicious.

1 Preheat the oven to 200°C/180°C fan/Gas 6.
2 Put the pecans in a baking tray and place in the oven for 5 minutes, or until well toasted. Allow to cool a little, then roughly chop and set aside.
3 To make the pancake batter, put the flour, baking powder and caster sugar into a bowl. Make a well in the centre, then add the egg, milk, melted butter and salt and whisk together until smooth. Set aside until needed.
4 Peel and core the apples, then cut them into thick slices.
5 Place a non-stick frying pan over a high heat and add 50g of the butter. When melted, add the apples and cook until they begin to brown. Pour in the Calvados and carefully flambé it in the pan. When the flames die down, add the vanilla paste and muscovado sugar and mix well. Pour in the cream, stir well, then remove from the heat.
6 Place two non-stick frying pans over a medium–high heat and rub with a little of the remaining butter. Add 2 or 3 large spoonfuls of the batter to the pans, depending on size, and cook for a minute or so on each side, until lightly browned. Transfer to a baking tray and keep warm while you make the rest of the pancakes (there should be 12–16 in total).
7 Put the apples back over a high heat and cook until the caramel sauce thickens.
8 Serve the pancakes in stacks of 3 or 4 on each plate. Top with apples and smother in caramel sauce. Sprinkle with the toasted pecans and serve with a big scoop of vanilla ice cream on the side.

Choc Nut Vegan Mousse

Serves 4–6

150g ripe avocados (about 2 fruits)
150g bananas (about 2 fruits)
1 tbsp vanilla extract
30ml cold strong black coffee
50g peanut butter
80g good-quality cocoa powder
80ml maple syrup
Generous pinch of sea salt
60g salted roasted peanuts, roughly
   chopped
Large handful of caramel popcorn,
   to serve

I know it sounds crazy to make a pudding with avocado, but if you want to create a vegan mousse that has a silky, creamy texture without using eggs or cream, a ripe avo is the perfect ingredient. It also has the added bonus of being extremely good for you, so this rich, indulgent chocolate pudding is guilt-free... well, almost.

1 Scoop the avocado flesh into a large food processor.
2 Peel the bananas, break them into large chunks and add to the processor. Add the vanilla, coffee, peanut butter, cocoa powder, maple syrup and salt and blend until smooth.
3 Taste the mousse and add a little more salt, as necessary.
4 Sprinkle in half the peanuts and blend for a few more seconds.
5 Spoon the mousse into small bowls and sprinkle with the remaining nuts. Crumble a few pieces of caramel popcorn over each bowl before serving.

Flourless Chocolate and Raspberry Pots

Serves 4

120g dark chocolate chips (80% cocoa solids)

3 large eggs

100g caster sugar

Seeds from 1 vanilla pod

50g ground almonds

25g good-quality cocoa powder, plus extra for dusting

200g fresh raspberries, plus extra to serve

4 tsp crème de cacao or raspberry liqueur

These delicious mini chocolate–almond puddings have fresh raspberries steeped in liqueur hidden at the bottom of the pots for a boozy, fruity surprise. As they are made with ground almonds rather than flour, they are gluten free and have a dense, moist texture that I really love. Serve with a few extra fresh raspberries and a drizzle of cream for chocolate pudding perfection.

1. Preheat the oven to 200°C/180°C fan/Gas 6.
2. Bring a kettle of water to the boil.
3. Put the chocolate into a small heatproof bowl and place in the microwave. Heat on high for 20 seconds, then stir and return to the microwave for another 20 seconds. Repeat the heating and stirring until the chocolate has melted. Leave to cool.
4. Separate the eggs into two bowls. Add half the sugar to the whites and beat with an electric whisk until stiff peaks form.
5. Add the remaining sugar and the vanilla seeds to the egg yolks. Beat with the electric whisk until light and fluffy. Add the melted chocolate, ground almonds, cocoa powder and a spoonful of the egg whites and beat until well combined. Gently fold in the remaining whites, being careful not to knock out all the air.
6. Divide the raspberries between four 200ml ramekins. Add a teaspoonful of liqueur to each one, then gently spoon the chocolate mixture evenly over the fruit.
7. Put all four ramekins into a small roasting tray and pour in just enough boiling water to come 2.5cm up the sides. Place on the middle shelf of the oven for 12 minutes.
8. When ready, serve immediately with a dusting of cocoa powder and a few extra raspberries.

Dark Chocolate and Coffee Mousse

Serves 4–6

300g dark chocolate (70% cocoa
   solids)
300ml whipping cream
125ml warm black coffee
6 egg yolks
1 tbsp honey
40g chocolate-coated coffee beans,
   lightly crushed, to serve

If you have more time...
... allow these mousses to set
in the fridge for an hour before
serving.

This is the perfect ending to a great meal – an after-dinner coffee and chocolate rolled into one! If you like things particularly dark and bitter, leave out the honey, or add a little extra if you prefer things sweeter. The mousse is delicious served immediately while still warm, but you can also put it in the fridge to allow it to cool and set.

1 Bring half a kettle of water to the boil. Pour it into a saucepan and bring to a very gentle simmer.
2 Break the chocolate into pieces and place in a heatproof bowl. Sit the bowl over the pan without it actually touching the water and allow the chocolate to melt. Set aside.
3 Pour the cream into another bowl and whisk to soft peaks.
4 Put the coffee, egg yolks and honey into a second heatproof bowl and whisk them together. Once combined, place the bowl over the pan of hot water and continue to whisk over a low heat until the mixture thickens like custard.
5 Whisk in the melted chocolate, then allow to cool for 5 minutes.
6 Gently fold in the cream until just incorporated.
7 The warm mousse can be served immediately, or poured into individual bowls and chilled to serve later.
8 Sprinkle some of the crushed coffee beans over each bowl before serving.

Tiramisu Pots

Serves 6

450ml cold black coffee
50ml coffee liqueur
18 sponge finger biscuits
40g dark chocolate (80% cocoa
solids)
1 tbsp good-quality cocoa powder,
to serve

For the mascarpone cream
250g mascarpone cheese
50ml condensed milk
250ml double cream
100ml Marsala wine

If you have more time...
... put these pots into the fridge
for an hour or two before serving;
the flavours really come together
and they will be even more
delicious.

For this cheat's tiramisu, I use condensed milk in
the mascarpone cream rather than eggs, which would
be more traditional but also more time-consuming.
The milk brings a silky sweetness that goes beautifully
with the coffee and chocolate, and it still ticks all the
right tiramisu boxes for texture and flavour. If you're
entertaining, make these ahead of time and leave them
in the fridge until you are ready to serve.

1 Pour the coffee into a shallow tray and mix in the
coffee liqueur.
2 Meanwhile, put the mascarpone and condensed milk
into a bowl and whisk until smooth.
3 Put the cream in a separate bowl and beat with an
electric whisk until firm peaks form. Stir in the Marsala,
then fold the cream into the mascarpone mixture.
4 Remove the coffee from the freezer. If it's still not cold,
add a couple of ice cubes to the tray and stir until cool.
Take 9 of the sponge fingers and soak them one at a
time in the coffee for a few seconds. Break the soaked
fingers in half and place 3 halves in the bottom of six
serving glasses.
5 Using a fine grater, grate a layer of chocolate directly
over the sponge fingers. Add 2 tablespoons of the
mascarpone mixture to each glass.
6 Dip the remaining sponge fingers into the coffee one
at a time. Break them in half and add 2 halves to each
glass. Grate the rest of the chocolate over the sponge
fingers, then top each glass with the remaining
mascarpone mixture.
7 Before serving, use a small tea strainer to dust cocoa
powder over the surface.

Index

Page numbers in italics refer to photographs

A

almond, spiced peach, apple and almond crumble *222*, 223

anchovy 28, 135

    anchovy tapenade with ciabatta toasts *200*, 201

apple 235

    Calvados toffee apple pancakes 236, *237*

    celeriac and apple soup with crushed walnuts *22*, 23

    roast pork chops with crushed Charlotte potatoes and lettuce and apple salad 132, *133*

    spiced peach, apple and almond crumble *222*, 223

asparagus 44, 154

    halloumi, asparagus and green bean salad 32, *33*

    pea, basil and goat's cheese omelette with shaved asparagus and rocket salad 162, *163*

aubergine, warm aubergine, tomato and burrata *30*, 31

avocado 107, 239

    corn and courgette fritters with tomato, avocado and rocket salad *156*, 157

B

baby corn 68, 154, 158

bacon cheeseburgers with pickled cucumber burger sauce *110*, 111

bacon lardons 28, 132

balsamic glaze, mustard and herb meatballs with balsamic glaze and Parmesan cheese 128, *129*

banana 239

    banana split with salted caramel chocolate sauce *226*, 227

beans 186, 190

    baked halibut with borlotti beans and tomatoes 48, *49*

    lamb rump with creamed cannellini beans *134*, 135

    see also green beans; kidney beans

beansprouts 36, 80, 96, 158, 161, 182

beef

    bacon cheeseburgers with pickled cucumber burger sauce *110*, 111

    Mexican beef and jalapeño quesadillas 120, *121*

    rib-eye steaks with peppercorn sauce *130*, 131

    steak tacos with pink pickled onion and pico de gallo *106*, 107

beetroot

    beetroot, thyme and goat's cheese tart with pear and rocket salad *152*, 153

    beetroot salad with whipped goat's cheese *34*, 35

biryani, chicken biryani *184*, 185

blood orange, radicchio and fennel salad *202*, 203

blowtorches 10

blue cheese dressing and buffalo chicken 84, *85*

bread 111, 128

    black houmous with pitta crisps 198, *199*

    fish finger sandwiches 43

    kale Caesar salad with garlic croutons 28

    saffron chicken flatbreads with minted yoghurt *78*, 79

    see also toasts

breadcrumbs 108, 141, 181

    see also panko breadcrumbs

broccoli 190

    see also purple sprouting broccoli; Tenderstem broccoli

buffalo chicken and blue cheese dressing 84, *85*

bulgur and lentil tabbouleh with grilled feta *188*, 189

burgers

    bacon cheeseburgers with pickled cucumber burger sauce *110*, 111

    lentil burgers *140*, 141

burrata, warm aubergine, tomato and burrata *30*, 31

butter, brown butter *18*, 19, *176*, 177

butternut squash

    quick butternut and chickpea curry 142, *143*

    spiced squash and lentil soup 24, *25*

C

cabbage 149

    juniper venison steaks with quick-braised red cabbage 116, *117*

cacio e pepe with Parmesan crisps *168*, 169

Caesar salad, kale Caesar salad with garlic croutons 28, *29*

Calvados toffee apple pancakes 236, *237*

cannellini beans, lamb rump with creamed cannellini beans *134*, 135

caramel, banana split with salted caramel chocolate sauce *226*, 227

carrot 36, 83, 149, 154, 185

baked sea bream with fennel, carrot and lemon *62*, 63

Moroccan carrot salad *204*, 205

pancetta-wrapped guinea fowl with glazed carrots and mustard sauce 100, *101*

cauliflower

cauliflower soup with brown butter and cheesy toasts *18*, 19

crispy chicken quinoa and cauliflower `couscous' with charred corn 190, *191*

roasted cauliflower with Israeli couscous, harissa oil and lime crème fraîche 150, *151*

celeriac

celeriac and apple soup with crushed walnuts *22*, 23

pork schnitzel with celeriac remoulade 108, *109*

Cheddar cheese 120, 141, 157

cheese

bacon cheeseburgers with pickled cucumber burger sauce *110*, 111

cauliflower soup with brown butter and cheesy toasts *18*, 19

truffle mushrooms with cheesy polenta *144*, 145

veal saltimbocca with marsala sauce 127

see also specific cheeses

cheesecake

cheat's cheesecake with macerated strawberries 228, *229*

rhubarb and ginger cheesecake pots 232, *233*

chicken

buffalo chicken and blue cheese dressing 84, *85*

chicken biryani *184*, 185

chicken ramen 96, *97*

chicken and shiitake noodle soup 20, *21*

Chinese-style ginger chicken with garlic rice 88, *89*

crispy chicken quinoa and cauliflower `couscous' with charred corn 190, *191*

crispy chicken thighs with romesco sauce 90, 91

double lemon chicken 92, *93*

Moroccan chicken traybake *82*, 83

saffron chicken flatbreads with minted yoghurt *78*, 79

Thai chilli and basil chicken *94*, 95

chickpeas 60, 83, 141, 198

quick butternut and chickpea curry 142

chilli and garlic prawns 64, *65*

Chinese rice vinegar 12

chipotle crema 107

chocolate

banana split with salted caramel chocolate sauce *226*, 227

choc nut vegan mousse *238*, 239

dark chocolate and coffee mousse *242*, 243

flourless chocolate and raspberry pots 240, *241*

tiramisu pots 244

white chocolate and passion fruit parfaits 220, *221*

choi sum 20, 115, 146

chorizo, Spanish chorizo rice 186, *187*

cinnamon ice cream sandwiches with winter fruit compote *234*, 235

clams, linguine vongole with nduja and cherry tomatoes 173

coconut cream 24, 59, 142, 161

coconut flakes 220

coconut milk 146, 161, 220

pork larb with sticky coconut rice 124, *125*

cod

fish finger sandwiches *42*, 43

miso-glazed cod *54*, 55

coffee

choc nut vegan mousse 239

dark chocolate and coffee mousse *242*, 243

tiramisu pots 244

compote

cinnamon ice cream sandwiches with winter fruit compote *234*, 235

pain perdu with summer fruit compote 224, *225*

cooking temperatures 9

cooking tips 8--9

corn on the cob

corn and courgette fritters with tomato, avocado and rocket salad *156*, 157

crispy chicken quinoa and cauliflower `couscous' with charred corn 190, *191*

scallops with creamed corn and pancetta *50*, 51

see also baby corn

courgette 83, 161

corn and courgette fritters with tomato, avocado and rocket salad *156*, 157

courgette fries *208*, 209

crab and courgette spaghetti 174, *175*

soba noodle, courgette and brown shrimp salad with tamari dressing 26, *27*

couscous
    crispy chicken quinoa and cauliflower `couscous' with charred corn 190, *191*
    Moroccan chicken traybake 83
    roasted cauliflower with Israeli couscous, harissa oil and lime crème fraîche 150, *151*
    tuna steaks with preserved lemon couscous 60, *61*

crab and courgette spaghetti 174, *175*

cream 220, 228, 232, 243
    chipotle crema 107
    mascarpone cream 244

cream cheese 35, 153, 228, 232

crème fraîche, lime crème fraîche 150, *151*

crisps
    black houmous with pitta crisps 198, *199*
    cacio e pepe with Parmesan crisps *168*, 169

croutons, kale Caesar salad with garlic croutons 28, *29*

crumble
    pistachio crumble 215
    spiced peach, apple and almond crumble *222*, 223

cucumber 36, 60, 80, 189
    cucumber pickle *54*, 55
    Korean-style lamb with sesame cucumber *118*, 119

curry
    Malaysian fish and okra curry *58*, 59
    minced lamb curry *122*, 123
    quick butternut and chickpea curry 142

D

dashi powder 12

dressings 28, 31--2, 35--6, 56, 80, 132, 189--90, 202
    blue cheese dressing 84, *85*
    tamari dressing *26*, 27

duck
    Asian duck salad 80, *81*
    pan-seared duck breast with pak choi and orange sauce *98*, 99

E

eggs 44, 96, 128, 224, 240
    burnt meringue with poached rhubarb 215
    corn and courgette fritters with tomato, avocado and rocket salad *156*, 157
    dark chocolate and coffee mousse *242*, 243
    pea, basil and goat's cheese omelette with shaved asparagus and rocket salad 162
    saffron mayonnaise 72

equipment 8, 9, 10

F

farfalle with brown butter, peas and sage *176*, 177

fennel
    baked sea bream with fennel, carrot and lemon *62*, 63
    barbecued mushrooms with fennel slaw and onion rings *148*, 149
    blood orange, radicchio and fennel salad *202, 203*
    squid and fennel stew 52, *53*

fennel pollen 12

feta cheese 157
    lentil and bulgur tabbouleh with grilled feta *188*, 189

fig tarts with vanilla and honey mascarpone *230*, 231

fish
    baked halibut with borlotti beans and tomatoes 48, *49*
    baked sea bream with fennel, carrot and lemon *62*, 63
    Chinese-style baked sea bass 68, *69*
    fish finger sandwiches 42, 43
    grilled mackerel with orange gremolata dressing 56, *57*
    Malaysian fish and okra curry *58*, 59
    miso-glazed cod *54*, 55
    pan-fried salmon with pink grapefruit hollandaise 44, *45*
    pan-fried salmon with warm potato salad *66*, 67
    roast hake with saffron mayonnaise 72, *73*
    tuna steaks with preserved lemon couscous 60, *61*

fish sauce (nuoc cham) 12

flatbreads, saffron chicken flatbreads with minted yoghurt *78*, 79

fries, courgette fries *208*, 209

fritters, corn and courgette fritters with tomato, avocado and rocket salad *156*, 157

furikake seasoning 12

G

garlic
    Chinese-style ginger chicken with garlic rice 88, *89*
    garlic and chilli prawns 64, *65*
    garlic and herb mash *212*, 213
    kale Caesar salad with garlic croutons 28, *29*
    moules marinière with wild garlic toasts *46*, 47
    wild garlic turkey kievs *86*, 87

ginger
    Chinese-style ginger chicken with garlic rice 88, *89*
    rhubarb and ginger cheesecake pots 232, *233*

goat's cheese
    beetroot, thyme and goat's cheese tart with pear and rocket salad *152*, 153

beetroot salad with whipped goat's cheese *34*, 35

pea, basil and goat's cheese omelette with shaved asparagus and rocket salad 162, *163*

gochujang chilli paste 12

grapefruit, pan-fried salmon with pink grapefruit hollandaise 44, *45*

green beans 51, 68, 87, 95, 127, 135

green beans with tarragon and pine nuts 206, *207*

halloumi, asparagus and green bean salad 32, *33*

gremolata dressing, grilled mackerel with orange gremolata dressing 56, *57*

guacamole, pea and mint guacamole *196*, 197

guinea fowl, pancetta-wrapped guinea fowl with glazed carrots and mustard sauce 100, *101*

H

haddock, fish finger sandwiches *42*, 43

hake, roast hake with saffron mayonnaise 72, *73*

halibut, baked halibut with borlotti beans and tomatoes 48, *49*

halloumi, asparagus and green bean salad 32, *33*

harissa 12

roasted cauliflower with Israeli couscous, harissa oil and lime crème fraîche 150, *151*

hollandaise, pink grapefruit hollandaise 44, *45*

honey 92, 99, 115

fig tarts with vanilla and honey mascarpone *230*, 231

houmous, black houmous with pitta crisps 198, *199*

I

ice cream

banana split with salted caramel chocolate sauce 227

cinnamon ice cream sandwiches with winter fruit compote *234*, 235

J

jalapeños, Mexican beef and jalapeño quesadillas 120, *121*

juniper venison steaks with quick-braised red cabbage 116, *117*

K

kale Caesar salad with garlic croutons 28, *29*

kidney beans 120, 190

knives 9, 10

L

laksa, tofu and vegetable laksa *160*, 161

lamb

Korean-style lamb with sesame cucumber *118*, 119

lamb rump with creamed cannellini beans *134*, 135

minced lamb curry *122*, 123

larb, pork larb with sticky coconut rice 124, *125*

lemon

baked sea bream with fennel, carrot and lemon *62*, 63

double lemon chicken 92, *93*

tuna steaks with preserved lemon couscous 60, *61*

lemongrass paste 12

lentils

lentil and bulgur tabbouleh with grilled feta *188*, 189

lentil burgers *140*, 141

spiced squash and lentil soup 24, *25*

lettuce 28, 36, 111, 190

roast pork chops with crushed Charlotte potatoes and lettuce and apple salad 132, *133*

spicy smoked tofu lettuce cups 158, *159*

lime

lime crème fraîche 150, *151*

lime mayonnaise 70, 71

linguine vongole with nduja and cherry tomatoes *172*, 173

M

mackerel, grilled mackerel with orange gremolata dressing 56, *57*

mangetout 115, 146

marsala sauce with veal saltimbocca *126*, 127

mascarpone

fig tarts with vanilla and honey mascarpone *230*, 231

mascarpone cream 244

tomato, mascarpone and pancetta rigatoni 170, *171*

mayonnaise

lime mayonnaise 70, 71

saffron mayonnaise 72, *73*

meatballs

mustard and herb meatballs with balsamic glaze and Parmesan cheese 128, *129*

saffron orzo with turkey meatballs *180*, 181

Vietnamese meatball noodle salad 36, *37*

meringue, burnt meringue with poached rhubarb *214*, 215

mint 189

minted yoghurt 185, *185*

pea and mint guacamole *196*, 197

saffron chicken flatbreads with minted yoghurt *78*, 79

mirin 12

miso paste 12

miso-glazed cod *54*, 55

monkfish, Malaysian fish and okra curry 59

moules marinière with wild garlic toasts *46*, 47

mousse
 choc nut vegan mousse *238*, 239
 dark chocolate and coffee mousse *242*, 243
 white chocolate and passion fruit parfaits 220, *221*
mozzarella 120, 157
mushrooms 28, 146, 154, 158, 161
 barbecued mushrooms with fennel slaw and onion rings *148*, 149
 chicken and shiitake noodle soup 20, *21*
 porcini tagliatelle with pine nuts 178, *179*
 truffle mash 213
 truffle mushrooms with cheesy polenta *144*, 145
 veal scallopini with mushroom sauce 112, *113*
mussels, moules marinière with wild garlic toasts *46*, 47
mustard
 mustard and herb meatballs with balsamic glaze and Parmesan cheese 128, *129*
 mustard mash *212*, 213
 pancetta-wrapped guinea fowl with glazed carrots and mustard sauce 100, *101*

N
nduja sausage, linguine vongole with nduja and cherry tomatoes *172*, 173
noodles
 chicken ramen 96, *97*
 chicken and shiitake noodle soup 20, *21*
 Sichuan sesame noodles 146, *147*
 soba noodle, courgette and brown shrimp salad with tamari dressing *26*, 27
 tofu and vegetable laksa 161
 Vietnamese meatball noodle salad 36, *37*

O
okra, Malaysian fish and okra curry *58*, 59
olives (green) 186
olives (Kalamata) 32, 52, 201
omelette, pea, basil and goat's cheese omelette with shaved asparagus and rocket salad 162, *163*
onions
 barbecued mushrooms with fennel slaw and onion rings *148*, 149
 steak tacos with pink pickled onion and pico de gallo *106*, 107
orange
 blood orange, radicchio and fennel salad *202*, 203
 grilled mackerel with orange gremolata dressing 56, *57*
 pan-seared duck breast with pak choi and orange sauce 98, 99
orzo, saffron orzo with turkey meatballs *180*, 181

P
pain perdu with summer fruit compote 224, *225*
pak choi 68, 115, 154
 pan-seared duck breast with pak choi and orange sauce *98*, 99
pancakes, Calvados toffee apple pancakes 236, *237*
pancetta
 pancetta-wrapped guinea fowl with glazed carrots and mustard sauce 100, *101*
 scallops with creamed corn and pancetta *50*, 51
panko breadcrumbs 43, 87
paprika 12
parfaits, white chocolate and passion fruit parfaits 220, *221*
Parmesan cheese 28, 47, 51, 145, 162, 170, 177, 178, 181
 cacio e pepe with Parmesan crisps *168*, 169
 mustard and herb meatballs with balsamic glaze and Parmesan cheese 128, *129*
passion fruit and white chocolate parfaits 220, *221*
pasta
 cacio e pepe with Parmesan crisps *168*, 169
 crab and courgette spaghetti 174, *175*
 farfalle with brown butter, peas and sage *176*, 177
 linguine vongole with nduja and cherry tomatoes *172*, 173
 porcini tagliatelle with pine nuts 178, *179*
 saffron orzo with turkey meatballs *180*, 181
 tomato, mascarpone and pancetta rigatoni 170, *171*
pastry dishes *see* puff pastry dishes
peach, spiced peach, apple and almond crumble *222*, 223
peanut butter 239
 sesame and peanut sauce 146, *147*
peanuts 36, 239
pear 235
 beetroot, thyme and goat's cheese tart with pear and rocket salad *152*, 153
peas 123, 182, 185
 farfalle with brown butter, peas and sage *176*, 177
 pea, basil and goat's cheese omelette with shaved asparagus and rocket salad 162, *163*
 pea and mint guacamole *196*, 197
pecan nuts 227, 236
peppercorn sauce with rib-eye steaks *130*, 131
peppers (bell) 91, 141, 186, 190
peppers (padrón) 91
peppers (piquillo) 186
pickles
 cucumber pickle *54*, 55
 steak tacos with pink pickled onion and pico de gallo *106*, 107

pico de gallo and pink pickled onion with steak tacos 106, 107

pilaf, aromatic saffron pilaf 210, *211*

pine nuts

green beans with tarragon and pine nuts 206, *207*

porcini tagliatelle with pine nuts 178, *179*

pink grapefruit, pan-fried salmon with pink grapefruit hollandaise 44, *45*

pistachios 83

pistachio crumble 215

pitta bread, black houmous with pitta crisps 198, *199*

polenta, truffle mushrooms with cheesy polenta *144*, 145

pork

pork larb with sticky coconut rice 124, *125*

pork schnitzel with celeriac remoulade 108, *109*

roast pork chops with crushed Charlotte potatoes and lettuce and apple salad 132, *133*

sticky pork with Asian greens 114, 115

Vietnamese meatball noodle salad 36, *37*

potatoes 123

decadent mashed potatoes with three variations *212*, 213

pan-fried salmon with warm potato salad *66*, 67

roast pork chops with crushed Charlotte potatoes and lettuce and apple salad 132, *133*

prawns

garlic and chilli prawns 64, *65*

Korean-style prawn fried rice 182, *183*

salt and pink pepper prawns with lime mayonnaise *70*, 71

puff pastry dishes

beetroot, thyme and goat's cheese tart with pear and rocket salad 153

cinnamon ice cream sandwiches with winter fruit compote 235

fig tarts with vanilla and honey mascarpone *230*, 231

purple sprouting broccoli 48, 112, 135

Q

quesadillas, Mexican beef and jalapeño quesadillas 120, *121*

quinoa, crispy chicken quinoa and cauliflower `couscous' with charred corn 190, *191*

R

radicchio, blood orange and fennel salad *202*, 203

ramen, chicken ramen 96, *97*

ras-el-hanout 12--13

raspberry 224

flourless chocolate and raspberry pots 240, *241*

red cabbage 149

juniper venison steaks with quick-braised red cabbage 116, *117*

remoulade, pork schnitzel with celeriac remoulade 108, *109*

rhubarb

burnt meringue with poached rhubarb *214*, 215

rhubarb and ginger cheesecake pots 232, *233*

rib-eye steaks with peppercorn sauce *130*, 131

rice

aromatic saffron pilaf 210, *211*

chicken biryani *184*, 185

Chinese-style ginger chicken with garlic rice 88, *89*

Korean-style prawn fried rice 182, *183*

pork larb with sticky coconut rice 124, *125*

Spanish chorizo rice 186, *187*

Thai chilli and basil chicken 95

rigatoni, tomato, mascarpone and pancetta rigatoni 170, *171*

rocket 31

beetroot, thyme and goat's cheese tart with pear and rocket salad *152*, 153

corn and courgette fritters with tomato, avocado and rocket salad *156*, 157

pea, basil and goat's cheese omelette with shaved asparagus and rocket salad 162, *163*

romesco sauce with crispy chicken thighs *90*, 91

S

saffron 13

aromatic saffron pilaf 210, *211*

saffron chicken flatbreads with minted yoghurt *78*, 79

saffron mayonnaise 72, *73*

saffron orzo with turkey meatballs *180*, 181

salads

Asian duck salad 80, *81*

beetroot, thyme and goat's cheese tart with pear and rocket salad *152*, 153

beetroot salad with whipped goat's cheese *34*, 35

blood orange, radicchio and fennel salad *202*, 203

corn and courgette fritters with tomato, avocado and rocket salad *156*, 157

halloumi, asparagus and green bean salad 32, *33*

kale Caesar salad with garlic croutons 28, *29*

Moroccan carrot salad *204*, 205

pea, basil and goat's cheese omelette with shaved asparagus and rocket salad 162, *163*

roast pork chops with crushed Charlotte potatoes and lettuce and apple salad 132, *133*

soba noodle, courgette and brown shrimp salad with tamari dressing 26, 27

Vietnamese meatball noodle salad 36, *37*

salmon

    pan-fried salmon with pink grapefruit hollandaise 44, *45*

    pan-fried salmon with warm potato salad *66*, 67

salsa 120, *121*

saltimbocca, veal saltimbocca with marsala sauce *126*, 127

sauces

    burger sauce *110*, 111

    marsala sauce *126*, 127

    mushroom sauce 112, *113*

    mustard sauce 100, *101*

    orange sauce *98*, 99

    peppercorn sauce *130*, 131

    romesco sauce *90*, 91

    salted caramel chocolate sauce *226*, 227

    sesame and peanut sauce 146, *147*

    tartare sauce *42*, 43

scallops with creamed corn and pancetta *50*, 51

sea bass, Chinese-style baked sea bass 68, *69*

seasonings 12--13

shaoxing wine 13

shichimi togarashi 13

shiitake and chicken noodle soup 20, *21*

shrimp, soba noodle, courgette and brown shrimp salad with tamari dressing *26*, 27

Sichuan peppercorns 13

slaw, barbecued mushrooms with fennel slaw and onion rings *148*, 149

soba noodles, courgette and brown shrimp salad with tamari dressing *26*, 27

soups

    cauliflower soup with brown butter and cheesy toasts *18*, 19

    celeriac and apple soup with crushed walnuts *22*, 23

    chicken and shiitake noodle soup 20, *21*

    spiced squash and lentil soup 24, *25*

spaghetti, crab and courgette spaghetti 174, *175*

speck, veal saltimbocca with marsala sauce 127

spinach 96, 142, 185

squid and fennel stew 52, *53*

sriracha sauce 13

steak

    rib-eye steaks with peppercorn sauce *130*, 131

    steak tacos with pink pickled onion and pico de gallo *106*, 107

stew, squid and fennel stew 52, *53*

stir-fries, vegetable stir-fry 154, *155*

strawberry 21, 224

    cheat's cheesecake with macerated strawberries 228, *229*

sumac 13

T

tabbouleh, lentil and bulgur tabbouleh with grilled feta *188*, 189

tacos, steak tacos with pink pickled onion and pico de gallo *106*, 107

tagliatelle, porcini tagliatelle with pine nuts 178, *179*

tahini 119, 146, 198

taleggio cheese 127, 145

tamari dressing *26*, 27

tamarind paste 13

tapenade, anchovy tapenade with ciabatta toasts *200*, 201

tartare sauce *42*, 43

tarts

    beetroot, thyme and goat's cheese tart with pear and rocket salad *152*, 153

    fig tarts with vanilla and honey mascarpone *230*, 231

Tenderstem broccoli 55, 72, 95

tiramisu pots 244, *245*

toasts

    anchovy tapenade with ciabatta toasts *200*, 201

    cheesy toasts *18*, 19

    moules marinière with wild garlic toasts *46*, 47

toffee, Calvados toffee apple pancakes 236, *237*

tofu

    spicy smoked tofu lettuce cups 158, *159*

    tofu and vegetable laksa *160*, 161

tomatoes 52, 59, 107, 111, 120, 123, 185

    baked halibut with borlotti beans and tomatoes 48, *49*

    corn and courgette fritters with tomato, avocado and rocket salad *156*, 157

    salsa 120

    tomato, mascarpone and pancetta rigatoni 170, *171*

    warm aubergine, tomato and burrata *30*, 31

tomatoes (cherry) 27, 32, 64, 79, 107, 186, 189

    linguine vongole with nduja and cherry tomatoes *172*, 173

tomatoes (sunblush), tomato, mascarpone and pancetta rigatoni 170, *171*

truffle 19

    truffle mash *212*, 213

    truffle mushrooms with cheesy polenta *144*, 145

tuna steaks with preserved lemon couscous 60, *61*

turkey

    saffron orzo with turkey meatballs *180*, 181

    wild garlic turkey kievs *86*, 87

V

vanilla and honey mascarpone with fig tarts *230*, 231

veal

veal saltimbocca with marsala sauce *126*, 127

veal scallopini with mushroom sauce 112, *113*

vegetable stir-fry 154, *155*

venison, juniper venison steaks with quick-braised red cabbage 116, *117*

vongole, linguine vongole with nduja and cherry tomatoes *172*, 173

W

walnuts 153

celeriac and apple soup with crushed walnuts *22*, 23

watercress 43, 80

white chocolate and passion fruit parfaits 220, *221*

Y

yoghurt 84, 232

minted yoghurt *78*, 79, 185, *185*

Acknowledgements

However fast the recipes are, it still takes a great deal of time and effort to produce a new cookbook. I am, therefore, hugely grateful to the brilliant people at Hodder & Stoughton for helping me pull this one together with their customary enthusiasm, patience and dedication. Particular thanks go to editorial director, Nicky Ross, project editor Natalie Bradley, art director Alasdair Oliver and senior production controller Susan Spratt for creating the book and to Caitriona Horne and Jenny Platt for marketing and publicising it. It has been great working with you all again. Editorially, thanks so much to Camilla Stoddart and Trish Burgess for helping me dot my 'i's and cross my 't's – you've done a great job.

Thanks also to my publishers for putting together a winning creative team to make the book look so beautiful. I am hugely thankful to Peter Dawson and Alice Kennedy-Owen at Grade Design for the skilful art direction and beautiful design; Louise Hagger for the stunning photography; Nicole Herft for the knockout food styling and for her amazing attitude to hard work; and Alexander Breeze and Louie Waller for their wizardry with the props.

Thank you to James 'Jocky' Petrie and all the chefs in my restaurants who work tirelessly to push the boundaries of food development. I really appreciate everything you do.

I am so grateful to Rachel Ferguson in the UK and Katie Besozzi in the US for helping me keep to my busy schedule on both sides of the pond. I don't know where I'd be without you. Literally!

Lastly I'd like to thank my incredible family: my wonderful wife Tana and our five children, Megan, Holly, Jack, Tilly and new arrival Oscar. You lot are everything to me and I am grateful every day.

Metric/Imperial Conversion Chart

All equivalents are rounded, for practical convenience.

Weight

25g	1 oz
50g	2 oz
100g	3½ oz
150g	5 oz
200g	7 oz
250g	9 oz
300g	10 oz
400g	14 oz
500g	1 lb 2 oz
1 kg	2¼ lb

Length

1cm	½ inch
2.5cm	1 inch
20cm	8 inches
25cm	10 inches
30cm	12 inches

Oven temperatures

Celsius	Fahrenheit
140	275
150	300
160	325
180	350
190	375
200	400
220	425
230	450

Volume (liquids)

5ml	–	1 tsp
15ml	–	1 tbsp
30ml	1 fl oz	⅛ cup
60ml	2 fl oz	¼ cup
75ml	–	⅓ cup
120ml	4 fl oz	½ cup
150ml	5 fl oz	⅔ cup
175ml	–	¾ cup
250ml	8 fl oz	1 cup
1 litre	1 quart	4 cups

Volume (dry ingredients – an approximate guide)

butter	225g	1 cup (2 sticks)
rolled oats	100g	1 cup
fine powders (e.g. flour)	125g	1 cup
breadcrumbs (fresh)	50g	1 cup
breadcrumbs (dried)	125g	1 cup
nuts (e.g. almonds)	125g	1 cup
seeds (e.g. chia)	160g	1 cup
dried fruit (e.g. raisins)	150g	1 cup
dried legumes (large, e.g. chickpeas)	170g	1 cup
grains, granular goods and small dried legumes (e.g. rice, quinoa, sugar, lentils)	200g	1 cup
grated cheese	100g	1 cup